MW00810195

A SERIES OF LESSONS IN ISLAM

THE
Progeny
THE PROPHET AND HIS HOUSEHOLD

Sayyid Ali Al-Hakeem

THE MAINSTAY
FOUNDATION

Author: Sayyid Ali Al-Hakeem

Translated and Edited by: The Mainstay Foundation

© 2015 The Mainstay Foundation

Printed in the United States.

ISBN: 978-1943393848

To our guide. To our hope. To our salvation.

To our Prophet (s).

Contents

ABOUT THE AUTHOR

Sayyid Ali Al-Hakeem is an esteemed Muslim scholar, lecturer, and researcher residing in Dubai, UAE. Sayyid Al-Hakeem spent ten years studying at the Islamic seminaries of Qum, Iran. There, he completed his Advanced Seminars (a Ph.D. equivalent in Islamic seminaries) in Islamic Jurisprudence and Thought. He also received a Master's degree in Islamic Thought from the Islamic University of Lebanon. Sayyid Al-Hakeem has dedicated the past twenty-two years of his life to service of the Muslim community in different capacities. He serves as a resident scholar in the Imam Hassan Mosque, Dubai. He is the Chair of the Religious Committee and the religious supervisor of the Charitable Deeds Committee of the Ja'afariya Endowment Charitable Council of Dubai.

TRANSLATOR'S PREFACE

The task of translating Sayyid Ali Al-Hakeem's book was gratifying and enlightening. The book delivered precious nuggets of knowledge and polished pearls of wisdom in a style that is conversational and pleasant. This book is our attempt to pass these nuggets and pearls on to you in a style that is similarly conversational and pleasant. We thank the Sayyid for allowing us to benefit from this endeavor. We wish for him a life filled with scholarly attainment, in hopes that he will continue to pass along his treasures.

Here, we must humbly admit some of our biggest limitations. First, we must admit the great difficulty that comes with the attempting to translate the Holy Quran. Muslim scholars have pondered on the meanings of the holy text for centuries, and the meanings of its verses only grow deeper as time passes. The process of translation always begs us to find precise meanings for the passages that we translate. But when we encounter the majesty of the Holy Quran, we find ourselves incapable of understanding, let alone translating, its true and deep meanings. We turned to the works of translators who have attempted to do this before. Although no translation can do justice to the Holy Quran, we found that the translation of Ali Quri Qarai to be the most proper in understanding when compared to the understanding of the text as derived by our grand scholars. As such, we decided to rely on Qarai's translations throughout this book, with some adaptations that allowed us to weave the verses more properly with the rest of the work.

A second great limitation came with translation of the narrations of the Grand Prophet Muhammad (s) and his Holy Household (a). Their words are ever so deep and ever so powerful. We attempted to convey these passages to the reader in a tone that is understandable without deviating from the essence of the words of these immaculate personalities. We pray that we were successful in this endeavor.

Finally, we want to take this opportunity to thank you for your support. As students of Islam and as translators of this text, our greatest purpose is to please God by passing along these teachings to others. By picking up this book, you've lent your crucial support in this endeavor. We hope that you will continue your support throughout the rest of this book, and we ask that you keep us in prayers whenever you pick it up.

The Editorial and Translation Team,

The Mainstay Foundation

INTRODUCTION

In the name of God the Beneficent the Merciful

Praise be to God, Lord of the Worlds. May God send His peace and blessings to the most noble of His creatures, the Holy Prophet Muhammad (s) and his Holy Progeny (a).

This book, *The Progeny: the Prophet and His Household,* is a compilation of inspirational lessons and parables taken from the lives of the Grand Prophet Muhammad (s) and His Pure Progeny (a). Greater focus is given to the first five of the Immaculate Leaders – The Grand Prophet (s), Imam Ali (a), Lady Fatima (a), Imam Hassan (a), and Imam Hussain (a). Those chapters are followed by shorter chapters and lessons from the lives of the remainder of our Immaculate Imams, from Imam Ali Zayn Al-Abideen (a) to the Awaited Imam Al-Mahdi (a).

The teachings of Islam have one unequivocal goal – to allow its followers to pursue excellence. From that perspective, Islam places great emphasis on knowledge and learning. We can see this clearly in the verses of the Holy Quran. These verses give knowledge a special status that is unique when compared with other human virtues. God says in the Holy Quran, "*Say, 'Are those who know equal to those who do not know?' Only those who possess intellect take admonition.*"[1] God also says, "*Only those of God's servants having knowledge fear Him.*"[2]

The traditions of the Holy Prophet (s) and his Progeny (a) contain numerous similar admonitions as well. It is narrated that Imam Al-Sadiq (a) said, "*The Messenger of God (s) once said, 'Seeking knowledge is an obligation on every Muslim. Verily, God loves the seekers of knowledge.*" It is also narrated that the Commander of the Faithful Ali ibn Abi Talib (a) once said,

> *Oh people! Know that excellence in faith consists of seeking knowledge and acting in accordance to that knowledge. Indeed, seeking knowledge is a higher obligation for you than seeking sustenance. Your sustenance is pre-ordained and guaranteed. Your Just Lord has divided it amongst you and promised to deliver it to you. Surely, He will keep His promise. [On the other hand,] knowledge is protected by its keepers. You were commanded to seek it from its keepers, so go forth and seek it.*

Islam did not stop at admonitions and theories about knowledge and learning. Instead, it created opportunities and enabled conditions that would foster learning, research, and study. Amongst these was the establishment of Friday prayers – God says in the Quran, "*O you who have faith! When the call is made for prayer on Friday, hurry toward the remembrance of God, and leave all business. That is better for you, should you know.*"[3] One of the important pillars of this ritual is its sermon,

---

[1] The Holy Quran. Chapter 39 [Arabic: *Al-Zumar*]. Verse 9.
[2] The Holy Quran. Chapter 35 [Arabic: *Fatir*]. Verse 28.
[3] The Holy Quran. Chapter 62 [Friday; Arabic: *Al-Jum'a*]. Verse 9.

where the prayer leader must convey Islam's teachings, in addition to addressing all other relevant worldly and otherworldly matters.

Dear reader, this series of books is based on a compilation of Friday sermons that I delivered over the years, as well as lectures I gave at a number of commemorations and celebrations. Throughout such gatherings, I have been able to address and speak on a wide array of issues relevant to the Muslim community.

At the insistence of a number of dear brothers, I compiled my notes to write these books with the hopes that God will accept the work and that the benefit will spread to the believers. I tried to maintain the conversational tone of the original sermons in order to make the books more reader friendly. After a series of these books were printed in the original Arabic, a group of believers then insisted to have the work translated into English so that English-speaking audiences may benefit as well.

I thank God, the Exalted, for His infinite support and favor. I must also thank everyone who participated in making this book a reality.

I ask God, the Almighty, to take this work as an act of devotion for His sake and to accept it by His grace, He is surely the All-Kind and Magnanimous.

Ali Al-Hakeem,

Dubai, United Arab Emirates

.

PROPHET MUHAMMAD
The Mercy to Mankind

In the Name of God, the most Beneficent, the most Merciful

We did not send you but as a mercy to all the nations.[1]

One of the most profound events that took place in history was the passing of the Holy Prophet Muhammad (s). It represents such a significant transition point in the history of mankind, because the one who passed was the greatest human being to ever set foot on this Earth. He was the best of God's creation, the pinnacle of perfection, and second to none without a doubt. As God's last and greatest prophet, Muhammad (s) possessed divine authority over all of creation, by God's permission. As the Seal of God's Prophets, Muhammad was the final messenger between Heaven and Earth. Thus, his demise meant the end of prophethood because Prophet Muhammad (s) was the last of God's prophets. A new chapter in history was started.

As Imam Ali (a) washed the body of the Prophet (s) and carried out the burial rituals, he eulogized saying,

---

[1] The Holy Quran. Chapter 21 [The Prophets; Arabic: *Al-Anbiya*]. Verse 107.

May my father and my mother be your ransom [O Messenger of God!] Your death marked the end of what had not ended with the death of other prophets; the end of prophet-hood, prophecy, and heavenly messages. Your [tragedy] is so unique [in its gravity] that [remembering] it has become a source of consolation for [tragedies concerning] all others; and your [tragedy] is so encompassing that all are inflicted by it equally. If you had not ordered endurance and forbade impatience, we would have run out of our store of tears. Our ailment would have not subsided and this grief would not have ended. And that would have been too little [relative to the tragedy of your loss]. But this [death or sadness] is a matter that cannot be reversed nor is it possible to push it away. May my father and my mother be your ransom; do remember us before your Lord and take care of us.[2]

The prophet-hood ended with Prophet Muhammad (s) and revelation stopped with him. This naturally commenced the new stage in humanity's relationship to those that the Prophet (s) chose as his successors. He said,

Verily, I am leaving among you two weighty things, if you hold to them you will never stray after me: the Book of God and my kindred ('itrah), my household (Ahlulbayt). Indeed, the two will never separate until they come back to me by the Pond [of al-Kawthar on the Day of Judgment].[3]

This painful occasion reaffirmed the great role the Holy Prophet (s) had in the journey of mankind. It sheds light on

---

2 Al-Radi, *Nahjul Balagha*, 2:228.
3 Al-Nisa'i, *Al-Sunan Al-Kubra*, 5:45; Al-Tabarani, *Al-Mujam Al-Kabeer*, 3:66.

the characteristics and attributes that baffle us, showing us their necessity and importance on the world.

One of these noble characteristics that were vested in the Holy Prophet (s) was his attribute in being the mercy to mankind, where God describes his purpose in saying, *"We did not send you but as a mercy to all the nations."*[4] Every prophet and messenger was a mercy; however, Prophet Muhammad (s) is an absolute mercy. His mercy encompassed all beings and manifested to the whole world. In his exegesis of the mentioned verse, Ibn Abbas said:

> *He is a mercy to the upright and the deviant, the believer and the disbeliever. A mercy for the faithful in this world and the next, and a mercy to the faithless as a reminder of the punishment they could have attained. It has been narrated that the Prophet (s) asked Archangel Gabriel,* 'When this verse was revealed did this mercy touch you in anyway?' *Gabriel responded, 'I was fearful of the Day of Judgment, but I felt safety in your presence when God revealed to you the following verse in my praise:* 'powerful and eminent with the Lord of the Throne.'[5][6]

It is also narrated that the Prophet (s) said, *"I am a mercy gifted [to all creation]."*

This gifted mercy was not exclusive to any realm of creation but encompassed all of God's creation. It existed before the existence of any creature on Earth, including the Prophet (s)

[4] The Holy Quran. Chapter 21 [The Prophets; Arabic: *Al-Anbiya*]. Verse 107.
[5] The Holy Quran. Chapter 81 [The Winding; Arabic: *Al-Takweer*]. Verse 20.
[6] Al-Majlisi, *Bihar Al-Anwar*, 16:306.

himself. This mercy did not cease, nor will it ever cease, after the demise of the holy Prophet (s). It will continue on and people will feel its effects on the Day of Judgment. What mercy is greater than it? And how would it be any other way when God ordained it on his servants as such.

In discussing the Holy Prophet's (s) status as an absolute mercy, we must point to the different roles and stages of his mercy:

THE WORLD OF THE SOULS

The Shia School of Thought specifically, and generally most Muslims, believe that the Prophet (s) had existed before Adam (a) came into existence. There are a number of narrations that point to this issue. It is narrated that the Prophet (s) said, *"I was the first of people in creation and the last of them to be sent."*[7]

It is also narrated in the 'Narration of al-Israa' where God speaks to the Prophet (s) saying, *"You are my servant and my messenger. I made you the first of the prophets in creation and the last of them to be sent."*[8]

It is further narrated that God revealed to Jesus (a), *"O' Jesus believe in Muhammad, and command your followers to do the same. If it were not for Muhammad I would not have created Adam and if were not for Muhammad I would not have created Heaven or Hellfire."*[9]

---

[7] Al-Haydari, *Al-Tawheed*, 2:441.

[8] Al-Haythami, *Mujama' Al-Zawaid*, 1:71

[9] Al-Nisabouri, *Al-Mustadrek 'Ala Al-Saheehayn*, 2:671.

A famous narration relayed to us by Jabir ibn Abdillah Al-Ansari says, "I asked the Messenger of God (s), 'What was the first thing that God created?' He told me, *'God created the light of your Prophet O' Jabir, and then from it He created everything else...*"[10]

After including the above narration in its entirety, Sayyid Tabatabaei says the following in his esteemed work *Tafsir Al-Mizan*,

> *There is much meaning in these words... and if you were to give it some time in reflection and contemplation you would find it as evidence for what we have brought forth... Do not disregard these noble narrations as the creation of Sufis and their 'delusions' thereby placing them outside of the mines of knowledge and the springs of wisdom. For in creation there are secrets. Look at the scholars of nature in their efforts to unravel the secrets of nature ever since man went out to explore the world. Every time they would discover one thing, they would realize how much more they did not yet know. Imagine that, when the natural world is the most finite and limited. So what say you in regards to the worlds behind the material veils of nature and those are the worlds of light and amplitude...*[11]

It is enough that the truth of these noble narrations are proven by the following verse from the Holy Quran describing the Prophet (s) as the first of the Muslims:

> *Say, 'Indeed my Lord has guided me to a straight path, the upright religion, the creed of Abraham, a Hanif, and he*

---

[10] Al-Majlisi, *Bihar Al-Anwar*, 10:24

[11] Al-Tabatabai, *Al-Mizan fe Tafsir Al-Quran*, 2:121

*was not one of the polytheists.' Say, 'Indeed my prayer and
my worship, my life and my death are for the sake of God,
the Lord of all the worlds. He has no partner, and I have
been commanded [to follow] this [creed], and I am the first
of those who submit [to God].*[12]

The Holy Prophet (s) is the first of creation, the greatest
mercy for the rest of creation, and that is for two reasons:

First, all creatures, every good thing, came from the light of
Muhammad. According to a tradition attributed to Jabir, it
has been reported that Prophet Muhammad stated this.
Regarding the light of Muhammad, the report says, *"Then
[God] created from [the light of Muhammad] every good [thing]."*

Prophet Muhammad, then said

*Then [God] upheld [the light of Muhammad] in His
presence, in the station of proximity, as God wished. Next,
He made [the light of Muhammad] into divisions: Thus,
He created the Throne from one division; the Seat from one
division; and the bearers of the Throne and the residents of
the Seat from one division. As for the fourth division,
[God] upheld it in the station of love, as God wished.
Next, He made [the fourth division] into divisions: Thus,
He created the Pen from one division; the Tablet from one
division; and Paradise from one division. As for the fourth
division, [God] upheld it in the station of fear, as God
wished. Next, He made [this fourth division] into parts:
Thus, He created the angels from one part; the Sun from
one part; and the Moon from one part. As for the fourth
division, [God] upheld it in the station of hope, as God*

---

[12] The Holy Quran. Chapter 6 [The Cattle; Arabic: *Al-An'am*]. Verses 161-163.

*wished. Next, He made [this fourth division] into parts:
Thus, He created the Intellect from one part; knowledge and
forbearance from one part; and immaculateness and success
from one part. As for the fourth division, [God] upheld it
in the station of modesty, as God wished. Next, God
looked at [this fourth division] with a gaze of esteem, upon
which that light emanated. [From that light] dropped
124,000 droplets. Thus, God created from each droplet the
soul of a prophet and messenger. Then the souls of the
prophets breathed. Thus, God created from their breaths the
souls of the saints, the martyrs and the righteous.*[13]

For what mercy is greater than this mercy? In that the
existence of what is created is contingent upon Muhammad
(s). For if it were not for Muhammad (s) God would not
have created Adam and those that came after. God would
not have created Heaven or Hell. In essence, everything that
is in existence is indebted to the Messenger of God (s).

Second, he was the means to God even while he was in
those pre-temporal worlds. This is confirmed by what is
narrated to us in the events that transpired with Adam (a)
after he ate from the tree that God advised him not come
near. Our narrations tell us that the reason God accepted
Adam's (a) repentance was due to Adam's (a) prayers in the
name of Muhammad (s) and his Progeny[14] (a). This has been
narrated across both major schools of thought. In regards to

[13] Al-Majlisi, *Bihar Al-Anwar*, 25:22

[14] The word "Progeny" is used in this book as a reference to the family of the
Holy Prophet (s). This includes his daughter Lady Fatima Al-Zahraa (a), his son-
in-law Imam Ali ibn Abi Talib (a) and the eleven Imams that followed from the
lineage of Fatima (a) and Ali (a).

narrators from the Sunni school of thought, specifically, Sayyid Ahmad Zaini Dahlan said,

> ... *And the narration of Adam's beseeching of the Prophet (s) is relayed by Al-Beyhaqi in his book entitled 'Dala'il Al-Nubuwwa' to which Al-Hafith Al-thahabi said: 'I recommend this book, for it is all guidance and light.' Al-Beyhaqi relays a narration from Umar ibn Al-Khattab who said that the Prophet (s) said,* 'When Adam (a) committed his mistake, he said: O' Lord, I ask you by the right of Muhammad (s) that you forgive me. God replied: O' Adam how did you know Muhammad (s) and I did not create him yet? Adam said: O' Lord, when you created me I lifted my head and gazed upon your throne only to see the words 'there is no god but God and Muhammad is the Messenger of God' written on it. Then I knew that you would not add to your name except the most beloved of your creation to you. God replied: You have spoken the truth Adam, he is the most beloved of my creation. If you ask me by his right I shall grant you repentance, and if it were not for Muhammad (s) I would not have created you.[15]

The greatest of God's creation, and the first of His creation, was God's Prophet Muhammad (s). Every good was created from his light; thus, everything was created from his light because everything that God created is good. Prophet Muhammad (s) is the grand mercy of God. Therefore, the

---

[15] Dahlan, *Al-Durar Al-Sunniyya*, 1:9. Citing *Dala'il Al-Nubuwwa* by Al-Beyhaqi, 5:489

longing to return to God comes by way of his mercy, which is Muhammad (s). And what mercy is greater than successfully reaching God.

THIS WORLD

Now, in regards to the Prophet (s) being the greatest mercy of God to all nations in this world – that is clarified through the following points:

He is the Axis of Divine Guidance

There is no doubt that the greatest message revealed to humanity was the message of Islam. The message of Islam is the continuation and seal of the previous divine messages that came to mankind, and will remain as the principal system of law and belief to mankind until the Day of Judgment. The Holy Prophet (s) is the one who came with this grand message and endured the trials, tribulations, and hurt that came with delivering the message. In this regard, the Prophet (s) said, *"No one has been hurt the way I have been hurt."* He sacrificed, endured, and went through so much pain for the sole purpose of bringing people out of the darkness and into the light. He was the teacher, the guide, and the cleanser for people. *"It is He who sent to the unlettered [people] an apostle from among themselves, to recite to them His signs, to purify them, and to teach them the Book and wisdom, and earlier they had indeed been in manifest error."*[16] He was the one who came with guidance from God, *"It is He who has sent His*

---

[16] The Holy Quran. Chapter 62 [Friday; Arabic: *Al-Jum'a*]. Verse 2.

Apostle with guidance and the true religion that He may make it prevail over all religions though the polytheists should be averse."[17]

The Holy Quran proves this truth and shows the people that Prophet Muhammad (s) was not sent except as a mercy to the nations: *"We did not send you but as a mercy to all the nations."*[18] For he was sent to all of mankind, be they disbelievers or believers. The believer will benefit from this mercy and its blessings and take from what it has to give. The disbeliever, through his wrong choices, will forbid himself from receiving the mercy and the blessings that comes with the mercy that is Muhammad (s).

Security for the People of Earth

Punishment descending upon the people that disbelieved in their prophets is a reality spoken of in the Holy Quran. When God sends a prophet to a nation, if such a people do not heed to the guidance of that prophet and disobey his godly commandments then divine punishment is inevitable. The Holy Quran mentions a number of stories of prophets and their people. The people of Noah received the punishment of the flood after Noah had grown tired of so many years of calling them to faith and was met only by their insistent rejection. The same can be said for the peoples of Lot, Jethro, the companions of Salih, Hud, and other nations. This translates that it is from divine tradition that punishment will fall upon the nations that disbelieve in God. With the presence of the Holy Prophet, however, the Holy Quran specifically states that God's punishment will not fall on the people of Earth. *"But God will not punish them*

[17] The Holy Quran. Chapter 61 [The Ranks; Arabic: *Al-Saff*]. Verse 9.
[18] The Holy Quran. Chapter 21 [The Prophets; Arabic: *Al-Anbiya*]. Verse 107.

14

while you are in their midst, nor will God punish them while they plead for forgiveness."[19]

Ibn Abbas commented on the verse, "*We did not send you but as a mercy to all the nations,*" in saying the following: "He is a mercy to the upright and the deviant, the believer and the disbeliever. A mercy for the faithful in this world and the next, and a mercy to the faithless as a reminder of the punishment they could have attained."[20]

The Door of Returning to God

The Prophet (s) is the door to God, by which people seek to have their sins forgiven and their repentance accepted. God made his Prophet (s) a reason and a means for accepting the repentance of his creation. God said,

> *We did not send any apostle but to be obeyed by God's leave. Had they, when they wronged themselves, come to you and pleaded to God for forgiveness, and the Apostle had pleaded for them [to God] for forgiveness, they would have surely found God all-clement, all-merciful.*[21]

For if a person wishes to return to God, the way to his Lord is through the Noble Prophet (s). Coming by way of Prophet Muhammad (s) is a reason and a means for God's acceptance of our repentance.

---

[19] The Holy Quran. Chapter 8 [The Spoils of War; Arabic: *Al-Anfal*]. Verse 33.
[20] Al-Majlisi, *Bihar Al-Anwar*, 16:306.
[21] The Holy Quran. Chapter 4 [The Women; Arabic: *Al-Nisaa*]. Verse 64.

PURGATORY

We believe in the world of Barzakh, or Purgatory, which is a world that exists between this life and the hereafter. When a person dies his connection to this world does not discontinue, there is a sort of link and influence between the world and man. Take the example of the Holy Prophet (s) when he addressed the fallen soldiers who lay dead on the battlefield of Badr, "*O' people of Qulayb! 'Utba ibn Rubay'ah, Shayba ibn Rubay'ah, Umiyah ibn Khalaf, Aba Jahal... have you found the promise of your Lord to be true? I found the promise of my Lord as true.*" Watching the Prophet speak to the lifeless bodies his companions said, "O' Messenger of God, do you call onto a people as they lay dead?" The Prophet (s) replied, "*You do not hear my words better than they do, but they are unable to answer me.*"[22]

We believe that martyrs are actually alive, rejoined with God receiving their sustenance from Him. "*Do not suppose those who were slain in the way of God to be dead; no, they are living and provided for near their Lord.*"[23]

If martyrs are alive with God, then what say you of the Master of Martyrs and the greatest of God's creation Prophet Muhammad (s)? Is it fathomable that the Prophet (s) is not alive and does not have an affect on our lives? Our creed is deeper than that. Not only does he affect our lives, he watches over our deeds and will give testimony to what he witnessed of God's creation on the Day of Judgment. And how could witness without knowledge or awareness?

---

[22] Al-Subhani, *Fi Thilal Al-Tawheed*, 435
[23] The Holy Quran. Chapter 3 [Family of Imran; Arabic: *Aal Imran*]. Verse 169.

The Holy Quran clearly mentions that the deeds of mankind are showcased to the Prophet (s) and he is a witness to it. *"...God and His Apostle will observe your conduct, then you will be returned to the Knower of the observable and the Unseen, and He will inform you concerning what you used to do."*[24]

The Prophet's (s) blessings encompass us all even as he lay in his holy grave. He is the mercy to all the nations as he walked the Earth or rest underneath it. The sanctity he held during his lifetime extends after his death. The blessings of *ziyara* (visitation) of the Prophet (s) is the same now as it was when he was alive. Our inspiration from Prophet Muhammad (s) permeate our entire existence because God's mercy to mankind, our Prophet Muhammad (s), will never perish.

The role of the Prophet (s) in the repentance of sinners has not changed after his death – this mercy is ongoing and by God's will it will not be depleted. A large number of scholars, like Ibn 'Asakir and Ibn Al-Jouzi, narrate from Muhammad ibn Harb Al-Hilali stating:

> *I entered Medina and came to the grave of the Prophet (s). I visited him and sat next to the grave. Another man came by, visiting the Prophet (s) saying, 'O' Best of Messengers, God revealed to you the True Word which says:*
> 'Had they, when they wronged themselves, come to you and pleaded to God for forgiveness, and the Apostle had pleaded for them [to God] for forgiveness, they would have surely found God all-clement, all-merciful.[25]

---

[24] The Holy Quran. Chapter 9 [The Repentance; Arabic: *Al-Tawba*]. Verse 94.
[25] The Holy Quran. Chapter 4 [The Women; Arabic: *Al-Nisaa*]. Verse 64.

So I come to you my Lord repenting from my sins seeking this intercession...' The man then left. I fell asleep and saw the Holy Prophet (s) in my dream. He told me, 'Follow that man and tell him that God has forgiven him by my intercession.' *I went out looking for the man but could not find him...*[26]

THE AFTERLIFE

The Prophet's (s) existence as God's mercy to mankind continues to encompass all of creation until the Final Day. His mercy is continuous because it overflows from perpetuity of God. And whatever flows from God cannot be limited, lessened, or added to no matter how many days or decades pass. The mercy of the Prophet (s) will be apparent on the Day of Judgment by way of his intercession, where he will stand to be the greatest interceder for God's creation.

One of the highest reflections of God's mercy is that very intercession. Through God's vicegerents and chosen apostles, God's mercy flows to his creation. Just as guidance comes to humanity by way of God's prophets and vicegerents, His mercy reaches his servants on the Day of Judgment the same way. All Muslims agree, with the exception of a fringe group of extremists whose words have no value, that the Prophet (s) is the greatest of interceders; he is the possessor of the 'praiseworthy station' as described

---

[26] Al-Subhani, *Fi Thilal Al-Tawheed*, 603

in the Holy Quran, "*It may be that your Lord will raise you to a praiseworthy station.*"[27]

Perhaps one of the clearest illustrations of the Prophet's (s) mercy is shown by the following narration from the Prophet (s): "*God honored me by giving me a request. I disposed my request for the intercession of the believers of my nation in the hereafter...*"[28]

No one is able to do without the intercession of the Prophet (s). It is unimaginable that a believer is free from all sin, and all sins are deserving of punishment if were not for the mercy of God through the intercession of the Prophet (s) and his Progeny (a). It is narrated that Imam Ja'far Al-Sadiq (a) was asked if believers get intercession. The Imam (a) replied, "*Yes.*" He was then asked, "Does a believer need the intercession of [Prophet] Muhammad (s)?" To that the Imam (s) replied, "*Yes. Believers have sins and mistakes and there is no one that will not be in need of the [Prophet] Muhammad's (s) intercession on that Day.*"[29]

The mercy of Prophet Muhammad (s) is manifested at his position at the Pond of Paradise when he sees some of his companions that have strayed from his path. Despite this, he wishes to encompass them in his mercy. As it is narrated in Sahih Muslim[30], Sahal ibn Saad said, that he heard the Messenger of God (s) say:

> I am the guardian of the Pond of Paradise. Whoever reaches it shall drink, and whoever drinks of it shall never be thirsty again. There will be individuals who will attempt to

[27] The Holy Quran. Chapter 17 [The Night Journey; Arabic: *Al-Israa*]. Verse 79.
[28] Al-Tousi, *Al-Amali*, 57
[29] Al-'Ayashi, *Tafseer Al-'Ayashi*, 2:314
[30] A primary text of narration in the Sunni school of thought.

drink and whom I know and they know me. They will not
be allowed to drink. I will say, 'but they are from amongst
my nation.' The answer will be, 'you do not know what they
did after you.' To that I will say, 'Cursed is he who deviates
after my death.'

What crime did they not commit against the Holy Prophet
(s) and his household and progeny? And what favor did
they pay him in return for being the mercy of God upon
them, taking them out of the darkness and bringing them
into the light? He made the masters of nations after being
disregarded as the most insignificant of nations.

The Prophet (s) will stand at the Pond and see some of his
companions and people of his nation. He will ask his Lord
to forgive his people. For what mercy do you possess O'
Messenger of God? And what vast compassion do you hold
for mankind? It is not foreign for a heart like Prophet
Muhammad's (s) to encompass even those that would go to
betray him and his loved ones. Prophet Muhammad – the
man whose body would be bloodied by his own people's
transgression and ignorance – would lift his head to the
skies and say, "*Forgive my people, for they do not know.*"

THE PROPHET AND KNOWLEDGE OF THE UNSEEN

Knower of the Unseen, He does not disclose His [knowledge
of the] Unseen to anyone, except to an apostle He approves
of. Then He dispatches a sentinel before and behind him.[31]

On the 28th of Safar in the 11 AH, the Muslims were
devastated by the passing of their Prophet (s). They lost

---

[31] The Holy Quran. Chapter 72 [The Jinn; Arabic: *Al-Jinn*]. Verse 26-27.

their forgiving father, their loving teacher, and the greatest man to ever walk this Earth. "*I am the best of Adam's lineage,*" said the Holy Prophet (s). His words could never be contested, as he was known from his youth as the Trusted, the Truthful. Anyone who did not feel the burning pain of loss at the passing of the Prophet (s) is one who did not know him. If we knew the Prophet (s), his status with God, his virtue and excellence, then we would know what it meant to lose him.

The Holy Prophet (s) was the end of the chain of vicegerents receiving direct revelation from the Heavens. On that day when the Prophet (s) passed, that connection between the Heaven and Earth was seemingly broken. Such a disconnect would naturally cause discord and chaos amongst the people. It was the Holy Prophet (s) that was there to bring peace, order and guidance to the people. He connected them to their Lord. In reality, that supposed disconnect which would induce chaos did not occur, because the Prophet (s) left behind successors and vicegerents by divine order. These vicegerents would continue to connect the people to their Lord and serve as the link between Heaven and Earth. Nonetheless, there were some who wished to benefit from the former idea that after the Prophet (s) the people were disconnected and ought to fend for themselves in matters of guidance and religion. Thus, some misused the absence of direct revelation to induce doubt, deviation, and suspicion, despite the fact that the connection remained through the Prophet's successors.

And so it began. Calamities, trials and tribulations would fall on the pure Progeny of Muhammad (s). From the sorrowful demise of their forgiving and gentle father, whom they followed as the Messenger of God and knew better than anyone else, to the discord amongst the people towards the Progeny and their right to succession. Days and nights would not pass except that this family was a target of the piercing arrows of their enemies.

In reading and discussing the life and demise of the Holy Prophet (s), it would be beneficial to contemplate an important matter. That matter pertains to the Prophet's (s) knowledge of the unseen. In contemplating this point, keep two things in mind:

1) Given that such knowledge is a feature of the Prophet (s) and the Immaculate Imams (a), it naturally follows that such a topic would be brought up in reflecting over their lives.

2) The relationship between the Prophet's (s) knowledge of the unseen and the pain and suffering that he and his family endured. Wouldn't a person who knows the unseen have the ability to distance himself from suffering? Wouldn't they naturally choose to do so?

So, does the Prophet (s) actually have knowledge of the unseen or not? Furthermore, having such knowledge does he have the ability to distance himself and his family from tribulation? And if he did have such knowledge why didn't he try to evade the tribulation that he and his family endured?

KNOWLEDGE OF THE UNSEEN

Many verses from the Holy Quran indicate that knowledge of the unseen is a form of knowledge unique to God and that no one is able to delve into such knowledge. Take the following verse for example:

> *They say, 'Why has not some sign been sent down to him from his Lord?' Say, '[The knowledge of] the Unseen belongs only to God. So wait. I too am waiting along with you.*[32]

Likewise, there are verses that seemingly indicate that none of God's creation, including the Holy Prophet (s), has knowledge of the unseen:

> *Say, 'I have no control over any benefit for myself, nor [over] any harm except what God may wish. Had I known the Unseen, I would have acquired much good, and no ill would have befallen me. I am only a warner and bearer of good news to a people who have faith.*[33]

In another verse God says,

> *I do not say to you that I possess the treasuries of God, neither do I know the Unseen. I do not claim to be an angel, neither do I say of those who are despicable in your eyes that God will not grant them any good—God knows best what is in their hearts—for then I would indeed be a wrongdoer.*[34]

---

[32] The Holy Quran. Chapter 10 [Jonah; Arabic: *Yunus*]. Verse 20.
[33] The Holy Quran. Chapter 7 [The Heights; Arabic: *Al-A'raf*]. Verse 188.
[34] The Holy Quran. Chapter 11 [Houd; Arabic: *Houd*]. Verse 31.

From another aspect we notice verses that indicate that
there are some of God's creation that have the ability to
delve into the unseen like the verse we began this chapter
with:

> Knower of the Unseen, He does not disclose His [knowledge
> of the] Unseen to anyone, except to an apostle He approves
> of. Then He dispatches a sentinel before and behind him.[35]

Thus, in taking all of these verse together and with the
support of our narrations tell us, knowledge of the unseen is
divided into two categories:

The Hidden

This is the knowledge that God has reserved for himself –
no one is able to delve into this knowledge regardless if he
is a prophet or an angel. Examples of this type of
knowledge include the time of the Day of Judgment and the
Soul.

Shared with His Prophets

This is the knowledge that God has allowed the closest of
His Prophets access to. Given Prophet Muhammad's (s)
excellence and perfection surpasses all of creation as the
best of God's prophets, the rest of creation that is able to
delve into the unseen is incomparable to Prophet
Muhammad's (s) knowledge and depth in it. And by that it
appears to us that these verses that discuss the particularity
of the knowledge of the unseen to God mean that God taps
into the knowledge of the unseen by His essence needless
of any medium or channel.

---

35 The Holy Quran. Chapter 72 [The Jinn; Arabic: *Al-Jinn*]. Verse 26-27.

Furthermore, the verses that say that none of God's creation can delve into that knowledge basically tell us that no one can tap into the knowledge of the unseen that is particular to the essence of God alone. In other words, the creation cannot delve into the unseen independently. Thus, if God gives permission to his creation, like the Prophet (s) in the verse mentioned above, what would be the problem? Through the Holy Quran and historical accounts of the Prophet's (s) life we know that the Prophet (s) informed the Muslims of a number of things that were particular to the knowledge of the unseen, like the events that would take place at the end of times.

So what would be the problem if the Prophet (s) had such knowledge with the permission and will of God? It is the knowledge that God chose to teach His angels and messengers. It is narrated that Imam Al-Baqir (a) said, *"Knowledge [of the unseen] is two: one with God that is hidden and untapped by anyone of His creation, and the second is what He taught His angles and messengers."*[36]

EVADING TRIBULATION

This matter relies on knowing the limits of the knowledge of the unseen held by the Prophet (s) and his family. Is the knowledge they have particularly limited or unlimited? The narrations on this issue do not all agree on one answer. Some narrations indicate that they know what was and what will be, and that nothing escapes them.[37] Other narrations indicate that there are limits to their knowledge, similar to

---

[36] Al-Kulayni, *Al-Kafi*, 1:147
[37] Ibid.

the narration we mentioned above by Imam Al-Baqir (a). Some scholars have taken this course – that the Prophet's (s) knowledge of the unseen is limited – like Sheikh Al-Sadouq and Ameen Al-Islam Al-Tabari.

Building on this opinion, assuming that the Prophet's (s) has limited knowledge of the unseen, he would not be able to evade tribulation for him and his family. But taking the first opinion – which is what is most widely accepted in our school of thought – tells us that the Prophet (s) was aware and knowing of all things that would take place to him and his family. Whether you say that the Prophet's (s) knowledge of the unseen is limited or not, history tells us that he did know about the tribulations and calamities that would occur. God blessed him with that knowledge. So then why did he not try to escape such pain and suffering and relieve himself and his family with the knowledge he had? This question can be answered by the words of some of our scholars.

> *Man's knowledge of good and benefit, like his knowledge of evil and detriment in future events, would be effective if it related to something that is plausible rather than being preordained. Take the example of someone knowing that if he were to be present in a specific place at a certain time on said day he will be killed without a shadow of doubt. Having this knowledge you would definitely choose to avoid that place and that time. However, if you had the knowledge that regardless of the place or time you choose you will die inevitably, you would not be able to evade the outcome no matter what you do. Thus, this person's knowledge of the detriment to take place would help him*

*practically in avoiding the detriment just as much as one
ignorant of what is about to take place.*[38]

Their knowledge of events lets them see the certainty of
their occurrence, as we expressly deny that their knowledge
is in anyway alterable. Knowledge of these inevitable
tribulations would not render them as bringing their own
demise even while knowing of the outcome. The Holy
Quran points to this:

*Say, 'Even if you had remained in your houses, those
destined to be slain would have set out toward the places
where they were laid to rest, so that God may test what is in
your breasts, and that He may purge what is in your hearts,
and God knows well what is in the breasts.*[39]

Moreover, there is another answer to this issue which is
explained in the third point below.

SOLVING PROBLEMS

Why didn't the Prophet (s) depend on his knowledge of the
unseen to solve the problems that he and his family faced?
Why did he not use this knowledge in addition to his divine
authority over creation that God bestowed him with? This
same authority was given to Prophet Jesus (a), with which
he used to revive the dead and heal the deaf, blind, and
leper.

There is no doubt that the Noble Prophet (s) is the greatest
of God's creation and thus this divine authority over
creation is at his disposal. His prayers are always answered

[38] Al-Subhani, *Mafaheem Al-Quran*, 3:447. Citing Allamah Tabatabaei.
[39] The Holy Quran. Chapter 3 [Family of Imran; Arabic: *Aal Imran*]. Verse 158.

by God. Through such power he could have lifted the many tests and trials faced by his family and nation through his answered prayers. In other words, he had three powers of the unseen that could have effectively evaded tribulation for him and his family: knowledge of the unseen, divine authority over creation, and his answered prayers. So why didn't he use any of these powers?

It is possible that one of the reasons for the Prophet's (s) choice to not use any of these powers to evade tribulation is related to his role as a leader. The life of a leader is characteristic of patience, forbearance, endurance, resilience and sacrifice. The leader endures to light the path for his followers and inspire them to persevere through life and endure their own challenges and tribulations.

If the Prophet (s) used his power to avoid his own tribulation then how could he convince his followers to stick it through and be patient through the obstacles and hardships they face? What kind of effective example would the Prophet (s) be giving his people? How could you expect patience and sacrifice from a follower when the leader does not show them the way and set the example?

God willed that the Holy Prophet (s) and his Progeny (a) would be the vanguards of patience and sacrifice. They would guide the way for the people and set the best example. They would endure the greatest trials and tribulations practicing the highest order of ethics. They would be the manifestations of excellence and perfection as a guide for those who would strive for truth and closeness to their Lord. When a believer strives in the way of his Lord, he has in the Prophet (s) and the Progeny (a) the best inspiration and example. The believer sees the Prophet (s) putting himself at the forefront of every battle and sacrificing himself and his family. The believer is thus inspired and rejuvenated to give everything he has in the way of his Lord, because his leaders did nothing less than that. The example of the Prophet (s) was an inspiration, a guide and a refuge for all. The Commander of the Faithful said, "When the going got tough and the battle was heated, we sought refuge in the Messenger of God (s)."[40] As he would return from battle with the Prophet (s), covered with wounds, he would follow the example of the Prophet (s) along with his loyal sons who were the pinnacle of patience and sacrifice – giving everything for God.

---

[40] Ibn Abi Hadeed, *Sharh Nahjul Balagha*, 13:297

BIOGRAPHICAL INFORMATION

Name: Muhammad

Title: Al-Mustafa

Kunya (Agnomen): Abul-Qassim

Father: Abdullah ibn Abdil-Muttalib

Mother: Aminah bint Wahb

Born: Friday, 17th of Rabi' Al-Awwal; in the Year of Elephant (570 AD)

Birthplace: Mecca

Died: Monday, 28th of Safar, 11 AH (632 AD)

Place of Death: Medina

Age at Death: 63

Gravesite: The Prophet's Mosque, Medina, Saudi Arabia

IMAM ALI
The Mountain of Success

In the Name of God, the most Beneficent, the most Merciful

Do you regard the providing of water to Hajj pilgrims and the maintenance of the Holy Mosque as similar [in worth] to someone who has faith in God and [believes in] the Last Day and wages jihad in the way of God? They are not equal with God, and God does not guide the wrongdoing lot. Those who have believed and migrated, and waged jihad in the way of God with their possessions and persons have a greater rank near God, and it is they who are the triumphant. Their Lord gives them the good news of His mercy and [His] pleasure, and for them there will be gardens with lasting bliss, to remain in them forever. With God indeed is a great reward.[1]

Remembering the martyrdom of the Imam of the Pious, the Commander of the Righteous Knights, the Prince of the Faithful Ali ibn Abi Talib (a), is one of the most heart wrenching memories in the souls of the believers. He is the

---

[1] The Holy Quran. Chapter 9 [The Repentance; Arabic: *Al-Tawba*]. Verse 19-22.

individual who dissolved himself completely in the love of God. He gave his entire life for God and spent his years, from his childhood to his last moments, in service and worship of his Lord. If you were to stand before the ocean that is Ali (a), you would fade before its majesty unable to grasp its unending shore and powerless to delve into its limitless depth. He is a man who gave everything he had of time, effort, dedication, money, and his own self completely and solely to God. Thus, he became the standard by which the pious are measured. Love for Ali (a) became the distinguishing factor between the believer and the hypocrite. As the Messenger of God (s) said, "*O' Ali only a believer would love you and only a hypocrite would hate you.*"[2]

We are unable to encompass the virtues and merits of Ali (a). His enemies tried to conceal the reality of his excellence and divert the spotlight of Islam on him. But even with their darkness, Ali's (a) light would only shine brighter.

> *What can I say of a man who his enemies hid his virtues in contempt, his followers did not make a show of such virtues in fear and caution [of persecution], and with all the secrecy and attempts to veil his excellence enough has been shown to transcend what lies between the East and the West.*[3]

We cannot do justice to the remembrance of the Commander of the Faithful in such a humble chapter. Our discussion here does not encompass even a simple drop in the ocean of Ali (a).

---

[2] Ibn Hanbal, *Musnad Ahmad*, 1:95

[3] Allamah Al-Hilli, *Kashf Al-Yaqeen*, 4

The remembrance of his death brings pain and sorrow to our hearts not only in regards to the oppression he faced, but for the nation that does not admit to his greatness – a nation that does not know its own value. It is painful to see Ali (a), the one who gave Islam everything, is killed in the name of Islam and in the name of the principles that Ali (a) was a soldier for. No one gave for Islam like he did, for he was the sword of God's Mesenger (s). He was the ambassador of the Prophet (s) and his brother, confidante, successor, and vicegerent. Abdulrahman Ibn Muljam did not simply kill Imam Ali (a), rather he killed virtue and faith itself. By murdering Ali (a), they killed prayer and fasting. They shed the blood of God's law. But they were heedless of God's words, *"They desire to put out the light of God with their mouths, but God will perfect His light though the faithless should be averse."*[4]

The oppression that Ali (a) endured cannot be captured by words. In what situation was Ali (a) not oppressed? The enemies of Islam targeted him for his undying loyalty to the Prophet (s). Even those who would later enter Islam but still had enmity toward the Prophet (s) would channel their animosity toward Ali (a). By degrading the Prophet (s) or attacking him they would naturally be accused of heresy, so rather than attacking the Prophet (s) directly they chose to assault the closest one to him – Ali (a). If not, what was the purpose of Ali (a) being cursed on the pulpits of the Muslims for over seventy years under Umayyad rule? The mere mentioning of Ali (a) threatened the Umayyads and their ruthless dominion. If they did not see Ali (a) as such a

---

[4] The Holy Quran. Chapter 61 [The Ranks; Arabic: *Al-Saff*]. Verse 8.

threat, and if he were not the complete human being that people naturally gravitated towards, the Umayyads would not have launched such ruthless campaigns to slander his name.

We are unable to address all the trials and tribulations that the Commander of the Faithful lived through, but we will address one particular injustice that he endured and its effects continue today. Some writers and historians accuse Ali (a) of lacking political skill and dexterity. They say that he failed in his administration of the Muslim nation in comparison to the caliphs before him and in comparison to his rival Muawiya. The mere comparison between the Imam Ali (a) and Muawiya is an injustice itself.

In this chapter, we wish to shed some light on this misconception and lift some of the injustice done by making the truth clear.

A MISCONCEPTION

It is important to understand where this misconception originated. The Umayyad propaganda machine, to which the Umayyad dynasty heavily relied on to build its own legitimacy, takes the lion's share of credit in fabricating this lie about the Commander of the Faithful. People that carried on the misconception attributed Ali (a) with being the "Imam of the Simpletons". The idea that he was not fit for governance and administering state affairs was pushed forward. They popularized the notion that Ali (a) did not enjoy the requisite political skillset nor did he have the cunning of a political mind to lead as head of state. They point to Ali's (a) short period of rule – 4 years – that was characterized by chaos, sedition, and civil war. They further assert that all this could have been avoided if Ali (a) were less rigid on some of his ideals and more flexible for political compromise. Take the following arguments as examples of compromise:

- What harm would it be to have given Muawiya governance over the Levant and then when stability is achieved he could remove him?
- And what harm would it have been to give Talha and Zubayr authority over Kufa and Basra as to deter them from waging the Battle of the Camel, which cost so many lives?
- And why did Ali (a) not simply compromise on so many other issues when it is only human nature to do so within the political construct of societies?

Ali (a) in the view of these spectators is not but a learned, pious, faithful, and brave scholar, except that he did not have political skill and knowhow like other caliphs and leaders.

DISCUSSION

To discuss this misconception a few points should be addressed:

First: Common Grounds

When we wish to compare two things there must be some commonality between them. It would be correct to compare, for example, between two buildings or two bridges because of the commonality that each shares with the other. We could say that Building A is a more impressive building than Building B because Building A interior was built with more meticulous aesthetic touches on an architectural level. Bridge B is better than Bridge A because Bridge B was built with better materials and is thus stronger and more durable. We are comparing what is relevant on the subject of the discourse. Both buildings have aesthetics and both bridges have durability, but one of each is stronger in that area than the other. And even more basic than that is Buildings A and B are both buildings and Bridges B and A are both bridges. We wouldn't compare the building to the bridge because in our discourse there is no relevant commonality.

Thus, if were to compare two things that had nothing in common, however, than the comparative study in itself would be wrong. Like our example, you would draw a comparison between the bridge and the building. Or on a human level, it would not make sense to compare a teacher to an engineer to evaluate who is more successful than the other. Their work is very different from each other and the way they are evaluated is also distinctive. In the same way, you would not compare Imam Ali (a) and Muawiya to one another in the matter of governance and politics, because there is no foundational commonality between the two in their visions of governance. Muawiya looked at the seat of power as a political ambition, a goal that he would do whatever was necessary to obtain. He made it clear to the people of Kufa after his peace accord with Imam Hassan (a), "By God, I did not fight you so that you may pray or fast, so that you may perform pilgrimage or pay alms, for you already do that. I fought you because I wish to rule over you. God has given me that despite your wishes."[5]

Muawiya inherited this political ambition and hunger for power from his father Abu Sufyan, who said, "Seize the day O' sons of Umayya. I swear by whatever you know me to swear by, I wish for you to take dominion and it will pass down to your sons. I swear to you that there is no heaven nor is there a hell."[6] For whatever price and by any means necessary – that was their outlook on politics and governance.

Ali (a) looked at governance as a tool to do justice, to lift oppression from the oppressed, and deter oppression. Otherwise, there would be no value in power and it would have no significance.

The very outlook on governance and politics differ in their essence as between Ali (a) and Muawiya. Thus, it would be fruitless to compare them to each other in governance. A person who sees power as an end is ready to do anything to get that power, while a person who sees it simply as a means would not care for the position if it did not serve to protect and promote his principles.

Second: Establishing Rule or Establishing Principle

This second point branches off from the first. Muawiya wished to establish for himself and his sons a dynasty of rule wielding the power of the caliphate. Ali (a) had no such aim and only wished to establish the principles of God. Thus, he did not care for political compromises and buying

---

[5] Al-Isbahani, *Muqatil Al-Talibeen*, 45

[6] Sharaf Al-Deen, *Haleef Makhzoum*, 192

people's loyalty for the sake of securing his position of authority. Muawiya, on the other hand, bought people's loyalty through appointments of position and wealth, case in point – Muawiya's agreement with Amro ibn Aas that Amro would be governor of Egypt. The Commander of the Faithful (a) was unwilling to strike such deals. He was unwavering in his principle that he would not buy people's loyalty no matter how small his support-base became. He was not even prepared to make some of the Companions advisory positions in exchange for their backing.[7] Rather we see his position as clear as day. He saw no value in rule if it did not implement truth and justice and deter wrong and injustice.

Abdullah Ibn Abbas said that he came to Imam Ali (a) who was in Thiqar (modern-day Nasriya, Iraq) and found the Imam (a) repairing his shoe. While working on the shoe, the Imam (a) asked Ibn Abbas, *"What say you of the value of this shoe?"* Ibn Abbas replied, "It has no value." The Imam (a) then said, *"By God, this shoe is more valuable to me than your caliphate, except for the fact that I am in a position to establish truth and forbid injustice."*[8]

The Commander of the Faithful's (a) sole goal in governance was establishing truth and forbidding injustice. That is why he refused to take the seat of power after the second caliph, because they wished to impose a number of conditions precluding him from accomplishing his goals of justice. He preferred to hold on to principle and would even

7 Review the Imam's words with Talha and Zubayr in *Nahjul Balagha* by Al-Radi, 2:184, sec. 205.
8 Al-Radi, *Nahjul Balagha*, 1:80, Sermon 33 when he went out to fight the people of Basra.

sacrifice his own right to speak out against the injustices done to him.

Third: Ali's (a) Political Acumen

The Commander of the Faithful was not heedless to the different instruments of political engagement and the devices employed for one to secure his interests. However, he refused to utilize such methods that were notably far from the correct path and teachings of the Holy Prophet (s).

The Imam (a) addressed this reality on a number of occasions. In one instance he said,

> *By God, Muawiya is not more cunning than I am, but he deceives and commits evil deeds. Had it not been for the reprehensibility of deceit, I would have been the most cunning of all men. But that fact is that every deceit is a sin and every sin is disobedience of God. And every deceitful person will have a banner by which he will be recognized on the Day of Judgment. By God, I cannot be made forgetful by ploys, nor can I be overpowered by hardships.*[9]

He knew all the tricks of the trade but was not willing to use them because they contradicted his principles that he never once swayed from. On one occasion we find the Imam (a) speaking to some of his companions that hurt him by not following him and heeding to his orders. He said,

> *By God, he whom people like you support must suffer disgrace and he who throws arrows with your support is as if he throws arrows that are broken both at head and tail. By God, within the courtyard you are quite numerous but*

---

[9] Al-Radi, *Nahjul Balagha*, 1:180, Sermon 200.

*under the banner you are only a few. Certainly, I know
what can improve you and how your crookedness can be
straightened. But I shall not improve your condition by
marring myself.*[10]

Ali (a) was more than capable to employ force or utilize
tricks and ploys to get people to follow him and establish
his own firm rule, but he abhorred such conduct. The whole
point of his rule was to manifest God's will and establish
God's principles, in complete opposition to what power
does to man in corruption and immorality.

Moreover, between Ali (a) and Muawiya, there are two
fundamentally different and contradicting schools on the
matters of governance and authority over people. Thus,
suggesting a comparative analysis on some basis of
commonality would be a fallacy and an indecorous endeavor
in every aspect.

OUTCOMES

Nonetheless, if we were to entertain the idea and compare
Ali (a) to his adversaries on the level of rule and governance,
would we determine success or failure for Ali (a)? We
believe and know that Ali (a) was completely successful in
his politics and governance. Consider the proclamation the
Commander of the Faithful (a) made when Abdulrahman
Ibn Muljam struck him with a poison-dipped sword in the
Mosque of Kufa. As soon as the sword hit his head while he
was in prostration Imam Ali (a) called out, *"By the Lord of the
Kaaba, I have triumphed!"* Could such an assertion be made in

---

[10] Al-Radi, *Nahjul Balaga*, 1:188, Sermon 69.

such a tragic state by one who was a failure? Only a man like Ali (a) could assume such confidence and certitude in a state like that. So we say it firmly that Ali (a) was not only a model of success in leadership and governance during his time but for all time. A number of points support this fact:

Realization of Goals

When we compare Ali (a) and Muawiya we ask if the two realized their goals that they set out to accomplish. Ali (a) was able to realize his goals completely. The evidence for that was the establishment of the principles of Islam and the preservation of the religion. No matter what the Umayyads attempted in distorting the religion and converting it into a tyrannical monarchial empire, Islam remained intact thanks to the sacrifices of Ali (a) and the Progeny (a). The principles and tenets of the faith were preserved, and the name of Muhammad (s) was protected and echoed five times a day throughout the lands of the Muslims.

Muawiya, on the other hand, whose aims were to rule and attain power for his bloodline was not able to realize his goals completely. Before he died he passed on the caliphate to his son Yazid, who only ruled for a few short years as he drove the caliphate into the ground by killing the grandson of the Prophet (s) and setting fire to the Kaaba. Yazid's son, Muawiya II, abdicated the caliphate when his father died and the seat of power was taken over by Marwan Ibn Hakam. No one else from the bloodline of Muawiya inherited the caliphate. Marwan's rise to power indicated a shift in Umayyad dynasty's lineage, from the descendants of Muawiya to the descendants of Marwan. The dynasty came to an end after nearly 90 years that left a legacy known for bloodshed, corruption, and tyranny.

So who can claim victory at the end?

The Position of History

History was not written by the champions of Ali (a). It was written by his enemies, or to say the very least individuals that were not his supporters. No matter what was tried in fraud and forgery of the events that took place, history kneels humbly before the sanctity, faith and piety of Ali (a). By all accounts, history cannot help but praise Ali (a) and expose the crimes and treachery of the Umayyads. Keep in mind this is even with the fact that most historians of the time were either supporters of the establishment or hired by it. So who claims victory here? Who does history determine as a failure and for whom does it claim success?

The Moral is in the Conclusion

The struggle between truth and falsehood is not limited to personalities or individuals, even if they played a big role in this battle of good and evil. We cannot judge the success or failure of a principle based on the life of one man that represented or opposed a particular principle. The work of men completes one another from generation to generation. What one starts is completed by the next. And thus, the struggle between Ali (a) and Muawiya did not end when they died. The vision and principles that Ali (a) held continues to fight against the ideology that represents Muawiya – an ideology built on sly tactics of corruption, blackmail, oppression and tyranny. These methods are still utilized and continue to battle the legacy of faith and strength in religion that Ali (a) sacrificed his life to establish. Success is not claimed but those who seemingly win battles here and there, it is in the finality of things. *"And the wrongdoers will soon know at what goal they will end up."*[11] *"And the outcome will be in favor of the Godwary."*[12] It is not who wins the battle, it is who wins the hereafter.

Establishing a Following

Of the signs of Ali's (a) success was his ability to establish a following that adopted his principles and followed his path. Against all the odds Ali (a) face, from oppression and civil war to propaganda and smear campaigns, Ali (a) inspired generation after generation to hold on to the teachings of the Prophet (s). People pray to God day and night to bring them closer to their Lord, through Ali (a). They pray that they are resurrected as followers of Ali (a) so that they may proudly stand behind the Commander of the Faithful (a) on the Day of Judgment. Ali's (a) name was raised next to the Prophet's in the call to prayer with a clear declaration to the continuation of the message of Muhammad (s) through the imamate of Ali ibn Abi Talib (a). What adversary of Ali (a) could claim such an honor? What opponent of Ali (a) could claim to have a following like Ali (a)? Is there a person on the face of this Earth that pleads to God and supplicates asking to be resurrected with Muawiya, Yazid, and the Umayyads? I do not think a person like this exists. If such a person does in fact exist he would either be ignorant or insane, because no sane individual would wish from his

---

[11] The Holy Quran. Chapter 26 [The Poets; Arabic: *Al-Shu'ara*]. Verse 227.
[12] The Holy Quran. Chapter 28 [The Stories; Arabic: *Al-Qasas*]. Verse 83.

heart to be brought up with the oppressors and tyrants of the Umayyads.

So who is triumphant and who has failed at the end? The answer is clear.

THE DAY OF GHADEER

Today the faithless have despaired of your religion. So do not fear them, but fear Me. Today I have perfected your religion for you, and I have completed My blessing upon you, and I have approved Islam as your religion.[13]

By far the greatest occasion in the history of Islam is that of Ghadeer. This is the day that the Holy Quran described as the day that completed the religion and God's blessing upon humanity. How could it be any other way when on this day the Prophet (s) called onto the Muslims with the greatest practice of religion – declaring allegiance to the Prophet (s) and his Progeny (a)? Our Immaculate Imams (a) tell us that nothing was called for like the call for this allegiance. It is the foundation upon which Islam was built and through it is the completion of faith.

If we are to look at religion as simply a collective of ethical principles and acts of worship, like many social and cultural systems already in place in society, we will not be able to understand the meaning of the completion of faith in this context. The revelation of the Quran ended and completed with the demise of the Holy Prophet (s). By the mere fact of the Prophet's soul ascended back to his Lord revelation ended. However, when we understand the religion we will

---

[13] The Holy Quran. Chapter 5 [The Spread; Arabic: *Al-Maeda*]. Verse 3.

realize that it is a continuous and collective movement towards God – such a movement does not stop. This movement cannot stop by the mere passing of the Prophet (s), and here is the important distinction. The Prophet (s) is the seal of God's prophets and the last to receive God's revelation; however, divine leadership continues and the connection between the Heaven and Earth does not cease. These divinely appointed leaders after the Prophet (s) take the torch of leadership and guide the movement the Prophet (s) led towards God the Exalted. This is the place and the significance of the Day of Ghadeer, also known as the Day of *Wilaya* (Allegiance).

Thus, religion could not be complete except by this guarantee of divine leadership that would be tasked with protecting the faith and guiding the people. Otherwise, if the religion were left to fallible beings it would definitely be corrupted and people would be led astray. The enemies of Islam at the time of the Prophet (s) thought that as soon as the Prophet (s) died, they would be able to rid society of its faith. Without the Prophet (s) the people can be misled. They neglected the fact that God's plan will always reign superior and He would have successors to lead humanity after the Prophet (s), starting with Imam Ali ibn Abi Talib (a). When they did come to this realization they were utterly demoralized. *"Today the faithless have despaired of your religion. So do not fear them, but fear Me,"*[14] because the Day of Ghadeer was what realized the completion of faith. It is narrated that Imam Al-Baqir (a) said,

---

[14] Ibid.

The practices of faith came down one after the other, and the
declaration of allegiance was the last that came down. God
sent the revelation 'Today I have completed for you
your religion…'[15] *and said, 'I will not ordain for you*
anymore practices, for I have completed them for you.'[16]

Indeed, this day was the day that religion was made
complete. His blessings were bestowed upon humanity. We
are immersed in God's blessings and his mercy flows
everlasting in our being from our first breath and until after
we die. Nonetheless, when we look at all the blessings in
life we find that the greatest blessing is the one that brings
us closer to Him – the blessings of escaping darkness and
entering the light. Such a blessing is different than the rest,
because it gives the individual the chance to be eternal – to
be everlasting in the grace of his Lord.

"If you enumerate God's blessings, you will not be able to count
them."[17] All gifts and blessings have an expiration at some
point because most of them are temporary in nature, except
for the blessing of divine guidance. Such a blessing
accompanies us throughout our lives and even after our
death. It is only expected of God's beneficence and mercy
that through blessing humanity with the perfection that is
Islam and the seal of prophets Muhammad (s), that He
would complete the package of blessing with the divine
appointment of successive leadership. That is what
happened.

---

[15] Ibid.

[16] Al-Kulayni, *Al-Kafi*, 2:289

[17] The Holy Quran. Chapter 14 [Abraham; Arabic: *Ibrahim*]. Verse 34.

The Day of Ghadeer is one of the greatest days of significance and celebration in Islam. It is not lesser in value than Al-Mab'ath Al-Nabawi (the Start of the Prophetic Mission). The Start of the Prophetic Mission initiated this blessing we discussed in regards to divine guidance, and the Day of Ghadeer's proclamation completed that blessing of guidance by providing a leader that would protect and honor that prophetic mission. The proclamation of this day made clear that all the responsibilities of the Holy Prophet (s) transferred to Ali ibn Abi Talib (a) except for receiving revelation and the title of prophethood, as Muhammad (s) was the last of God's prophets. However, the role of divine leadership (imamah), which the Prophet (s) himself assumed, would continue on through the person of Ali (a).

The Prophet (s) described to the people the relationship of his successors to the Quran in the famous *Thaqalayn* (Two Weighty Things) narration: *"Verily, I am leaving behind two weighty things among you: the Book of God and my progeny, my household. For indeed, the two will never separate until they come back to me by the Pond [of al-Kawthar on the Day of Judgment]."*[18] So what are these responsibilities that were to be assumed by the successors of the Holy Prophet (s)?

Delivering Divine Law

One of the most important duties of the Prophet (s) assigned to him by God is the responsibility of delivering to the people God's law. The Prophet (s) was able to deliver this law through the revelation he received as the messenger

---

[18] Al-Majlisi, *Bihar Al-Anwar*, 3:106

and prophet of God. *"And the Apostle's duty is only to communicate in clear terms."*[19]

The Prophet (s) would deliver every divine ruling that God would command him to deliver to the people, like prayer, fasting, pilgrimage, charity, and the rest of the practices related to worship and ethics. The Prophet (s) would practice the divine commandments himself, showing the people how to carryout God's law and inform them of their obligations. In this manner, the people felt responsibility towards this prophetic message and accepted what they were given and taught by the Holy Prophet (s).

Judgment

The second duty that the Prophet (s) had was carrying out the role of judge to handle disputes and establish justice between people. This duty is one of the most sacred responsibilities because judgment determines the outcome and dynamic of relationships between people. When a dispute between individuals takes place, people go back to the judge to settle the dispute and rule between them. Those are connected to God by divine representation, like the prophets and the imams, are the ones that hold this responsibility because they are the most able in this regard.

They are the most capable in understanding the disputes and the most qualified to have justice realized and deliver the proper judgments. Resolving disputes is of the work of the prophet, it is a divinely appointed position held by the Holy Prophet (s).

---

[19] The Holy Quran. Chapter 24 [The Light; Arabic: *Al-Noor*]. Verse 54.

But no, by your Lord! They will not believe until they make
you a judge in their disputes, then do not find within their
hearts any dissent to your verdict and submit in full
submission.[20]

Governance

The third duty that the Prophet (s) held was governance –
having political authority. The Prophet (s) is the highest
political authority because God designated him with this
task. In addition to being a prophet, guide, judge, and
arbitrator for the people, he is also the governor and ruler
over the Islamic nation – because he is the appointed
representative of God.

These three primary duties are particular to the Holy
Prophet (s) in his role as the representative of God. Note
that when we mention these specific duties, it does not
mean that his responsibilities were limited to these three
areas. The discussion of duties here is in the Prophet's
legislative capacity as the representative of God tasked with
the administration of humanity's affairs.

These responsibilities, though particular to the Prophet (s),
are transferred to Imam – divine representative – after the
Prophet (s), by the command of God. The Imam becomes
the deliverer of divine law, not by way of revelation
however because revelation stops at the Prophet (s). Rather,
the Imam shows and makes clear what the divine law is. He
teaches the people the law as it was taught and inherited by
him from the Holy Prophet (s). At the same time, he takes
on the responsibility of being the judge between the people.

---

[20] The Holy Quran. Chapter 4 [The Women; Arabic: *Al-Nisaa*]. Verse 65.

That is why we notice in the history of Imams (a) that the rulers of their time often went back to the Imams (a) to give judgment on complex matters of law. In those cases, the Imams (a) provided judgment and acted in their capacity as judges for the disputes and conflicts that took place both in civil and criminal spheres of law. It was common practice that the rulers of the time would defer to the judgment of the Imams (a), illustrating the unsurpassed knowledge, wisdom and judiciousness of the Imams (a) as they were consulted even by their enemies and oppressors.

The Imams (a) also inherited the third duty being governance. This duty is no less important the first two and even completes the previous two. When we go back to the narrations of the Prophet (s) we notice that he would emphasize this duty of leadership in Ali (a) saying, *"The most judicious amongst you is Ali (a)."*[21] The Prophet (s) would also say, *"Ali is to me as Aaron was to Moses, except that there is no prophet after me."*[22] In reference to the holy verse, *"You are only a warner, and there is a guide for every people,"* the Holy Prophet (s) explained it saying, *"I am the Warner and Ali (a) is the Guide."*[23]

Some may question the benefit of discussing the issue of succession after the Prophet (s) given that it was so long ago and history already took its course. They would be right if the issue was merely a political one or if it was only a problem faced by Ali (a) that was particular to his person. However, the issue of succession after the Prophet (s) is

[21] Al-Nu'man Al-Maghribi, *Sharh Al-Akhbar*, 1:91

[22] Al-Sadouq, *'Uyoon Akhbar Al-Rida*, 1:209

[23] Al-Khazzaz Al-Qummi, *Kifayat Al-Athar*, 163

beyond a political dispute and its effects extends long after Ali (a). Succession to the Prophet (s) can be addressed in two primary categories: 1) the historical problem and 2) the contemporary problem.

The Historical Problem

The historical problem is the issue of governance, was Ali (a) more qualified than the others for the caliphate or not? Given the plethora of clear narrations and historical accounts for Ali's (a) unmatched qualification and appointment to the position of leadership, the answer is yes. Nonetheless, the issue remains a historical one because it has already taken place and Ali (a) is no longer present, nor are his adversaries.

The Contemporary Problem

If the caliphate was merely a political position then being silent on this issue would have been possible. However, the caliphate represents the position of succession after the Prophet (s) and the assumption of the three duties that would pass from the Prophet (s) to the Imam (a). So if the rightfully designated person for the position did not assume the caliphate, it would mean that the Muslims did not have in the caliph the proper legislative authority to confer divine guidance after the passing of the Prophet (s).

This problem persists without being limited to a certain era or decade. Its effects continue on today and Muslims continue to suffer because of the lacking in proper legislative authority in the positions of leadership. It was because of this that Muslim jurists were forced to use *qiyas* (reason by analogy), *ra'iy* (opinion-based legislation), *istihsan* (preference-based legislation), and other tools for jurisprudence that do not have any evidentiary weight. They were forced to take this avenue in consideration of the fact that the Messenger's (s) prophetic mission lasted a total of 23 years ending with his demise. The Prophet's (s) words, actions, and decrees represented legislative authority over the Muslims; and thus, Islam's legislation was limited to those 23 years. With the expansion of the Muslims, the mixing with other civilizations and societies, and the rise of contemporary issues that were not addressed at the time of the Prophet (s), many Muslims felt compelled to resort to basing religious decisions merely on opinion, probability, and referring to the actions of the Companions.

We on the other hand, claim that after the demise of the Messenger (s) until 250 A.H. was a period of legislative authority that extended from the Prophet (s) – from Imam Ali (a) to the start of Imam Al-Mahdi's occultation. The Imams (a) after the Prophet (s) have what he had in authority, their words are equal to his in regards to proof and authority over the Muslims. Likewise, their actions are similar to his actions and their decrees are equal to his decrees. There is a tremendous difference between the amount of guidance and legislation provided to us from 250 years of divine leadership versus what was addressed in 23 years. The Imams (a) serve as an extension of the prophetic message in safeguarding the faith and delivering the divine.

Thus, this is an invitation to all Muslims to review the popular texts and research the topic of *Imamah*. This would help solve many of the jurisprudential issues faced in the sphere of Islamic law. It is important to keep this thought in

IMAM ALI

mind: not accepting the governance and political authority of the Progeny (a) should not result in also refusing their authority in knowledge and legislation.

BIOGRAPHICAL INFORMATION

Name: Ali

Title: Al-Murtada

Kunya (Agnomen): Abul-Hassan

Father: Abu Talib

Mother: Fatimah bint Asad

Born: Friday, 13th of Rajab 23 BH (598 AD)

Birthplace: In the Holy Ka'ba in Mecca

Died: Monday, 21st of Ramadan 40 AH (661 AD)

Place of Death: Kufa, Iraq

Age at Death: 63

Gravesite: The Shrine of Imam Ali, Najaf, Iraq

LADY ZAHRAA
The Perfect Exemplar

In the Name of God, the most Beneficent, the most Merciful

Indeed We have given you abundance. So pray to your Lord, and sacrifice [the sacrificial camel]. Indeed it is your enemy who is without posterity.[1]

When we remember the personality of Lady Fatima Al-Zahraa (a) we naturally become feeble and humble before her majesty and greatness. She is the personality that the Messenger of God (s), who does not speak out of whim and is himself revelation, described with attributes that he did not describe any other woman. She was a part of him, the light of his eye, and the fruit of his heart. It is narrated that the Holy Prophet (s) said,

> *Fatima is a part of me. She is the light of my eye and the fruit of my heart. The one who wrongs her has wronged me.*

---

[1] The Holy Quran. Chapter 108 [The Abundance; Arabic: *Al-Kawthar*]. Verse 1-3.

What makes her happy makes me happy. She will be the
first to follow me from my Progeny...[2]

It is also narrated that he said, "*Al-Hassan and Al-Hussain are*
the best of people after their father and me. And their mother is the
greatest woman of this world."[3]

Narrations like these are plentiful, illustrating her lofty status
with God and His Messenger (s). Those who assume that
the words of the Prophet (s) regarding Lady Fatima (a) are
expected merely because he was a kind father are mistaken.
Without a doubt, the Prophet (s) did have the greatest love
and compassion for his daughter Fatima (a). However,
those who limit the relationship with the generalization that
such love is expected for the mere fact that Fatima (a) was
his daughter is fallacious, for a number of reasons:

One, the Prophet (s) was a human being who had emotions
and feelings toward his family members. Those emotions
and feelings, however, were different in the fact that his
relationship with God dictated that his entire being would
be connected to God. In other words, his emotions and
expression of such emotions are only those that reflect the
will and perfection of God. In general, because of the level
of connection that the prophets have to God the quality and
level of their emotions also increase in proximity to their
connection to God. Thus, they will only love the things that
God loves and hate the things that God hates. This is
because their perfection and excellence is directly related to
the connection of their emotions to God. Think about it,
how could it be that God would expect a regular human

---

[2] Al-Sadouq, *Al-Amali*, 575
[3] Al-Sadouq, '*Uyoon Akhbar Al-Rida*, 1:67

being to connect his emotions and feelings to God, whereby he only likes the things that God likes and dislikes what God dislikes, and not have an even higher expectation of his greatest Prophet (s)?

> *You will not find a people believing in God and the Last Day endearing those who oppose God and His Apostle even though they were their own parents, or children, or brothers, or kinsfolk. [For] such, He has written faith into their hearts and strengthened them with a spirit from Him. He will admit them into gardens with streams running in them, to remain in them [forever], God is pleased with them, and they are pleased with Him. They are God's confederates. Look! The confederates of God are indeed felicitous!*[4]

On this basis, would it make sense that God would allow the Holy Prophet (s) to simply go about based on arbitrary feelings, sensations, and emotions? Would it make sense for the Seal of Prophets and the Best of Creation to behave like this?

Second, let us entertain this idea that the Prophet's (s) words with regards to his daughter Fatima (a) are merely articulated based on emotion. If we were to take this notion, with the fact that it does not contradict the prophecy of the Prophet (s), then why doesn't the Prophet (s) describe Fatima's (a) sisters – on the basis that those who bring forth this notion also claim that the Prophet (s) had daughters other than Fatima (a) – in the same way? Why would the Prophet (s) differentiate between his daughters if it was simply a matter of emotion, expressing love and kindness to

---

[4] The Holy Quran. Chapter 58 [Pleadings; Arabic: *Al-Mujadala*]. Verse 22.

his daughters? Is he not the Mercy to Mankind, why would he not express the same love to these supposed daughters as he did to Fatima (a)? *"There has certainly come to you an apostle from among yourselves. Grievous to him is your distress; he has deep concern for you, and is most kind and merciful to the faithful."*[5]

Third, if these narrations came about simply by fatherly emotion and sentimentality then there would be no meaning in connecting that relationship to God, whereby the Prophet (s) states that the contentment of Fatima (a) is the contentment of God and her anger is the anger of God. There are numerous narrations that point to this in slightly different wording.

"God is angry for the anger of Fatima (a) and is content for her contentment."[6]

In another narration, the Prophet (s) says directly to Fatima (a), *"God is angry for your anger and is content for your contentment."*[7]

If it were to be said that God is anger for the anger of every believer and is content for the contentment of every believer, then there would be no meaning to the words of the Messenger in specificity to Fatima (a) and his words would be in vain. We know that the Prophet (s) does not speak in vain or out of whim – he is nothing but revelation.[8]

There is no alternative but to say that Fatima (a) has a special status that is not enjoyed by anyone else except the

5 The Holy Quran. Chapter 9 [The Repentance; Arabic: *Al-Tawba*]. Verse 128.
6 Al-Shaheed Zayd ibn Ali, *Musnad Zayd ibn Ali*, 495
7 Al-Muttaqqi Al-Hindi, *Kanz Al-'Ummal*, 13:674, tr. 37,725
8 The Holy Quran. Chapter 53 [The Star; Arabic: *Al-Najm*]. Verse 3-4.

infallibles of the Prophet's (s) Progeny (a). Her contentment is the contentment of God and her displeasure is the displeasure of God.

Indeed, Fatima (a) has a prominence and eminence that cannot be encompassed or contained. Nevertheless, we should stand before this endless shore of greatness and attempt to catch some immaculate pearls. Let us stand awhile before this divine garden and swim in the fragrance of prophecy and guardianship. Let us stand before the holiness of Fatima (a) to learn from her life undying lessons and morals, asking God to bless us and make us successful. *"We would have never been guided had not God guided us."*[9]

PERFECT EXAMPLES

Islam is the great religion and system of faith that gave women a place of significance and respect in society unlike any ideology or faith before it. In Islam's view, a woman is the equal of man in humanity. In addition, Islam did not argue for the respect, ability, significance, and spirituality of women without pointing the practical good examples that prove this reality.

The Holy Quran offers some of these honorable and virtuous examples. Take the example of Mary (a), daughter of Imran and mother of Jesus (a). God referred to this honorable woman with the highest regard and praise of greatness and sanctity.

And when the angels said, 'O Mary, God has chosen you and purified you, and He has chosen you above the world's

---

[9] The Holy Quran. Chapter 7 [The Heights; Arabic: *Al-A'raf*]. Verse 43.

PROGENY

*women. O Mary, be obedient to your Lord and prostrate
and bow down with those who bow [in worship].* [10]

Another example is Asiyah, daughter of Muzahem and wife
of Pharaoh. She was the virtuous woman that stood defiant
against the tyranny of Pharaoh and believed in the message
of Moses (a). She showed that women are independent to
choose their religion and practice their faith. Women are
free to seek what is truth and are not obligated to follow the
beliefs, or lack thereof, of their husbands. So long as truth is
clear to her, she must heed to truth and is under no
obligation to follow the whims of her husband. This maybe
a given or something obvious in our day and age, but it
surely was not during the time of Asiyah. She became a
revolutionary exemplar for the faithful and her name written
in the Book of God as an example for the world.

*God cites an example of the faithful: the wife of Pharaoh,
when she said, 'My Lord! Build me a home near You in
paradise, and deliver me from Pharaoh and his conduct,
and deliver me from the wrongdoing lot.* [11]

Islam also has Lady Khadija (a) as yet another example of
perfection and excellence. She was the first beloved wife of
the Prophet (s), his sole supporter along with the young Ali
(a), and the first individual to accept the divine message of
the Prophet (s). Khadija (a) was a pillar for the spread and
expansion of Islam. The Muslims have not thanked and
appreciated her enough and she has a right upon every
single person who has accepted the faith. For the Holy

[10] The Holy Quran. Chapter 3 [Family of Imran; Arabic: *Aal Imran*]. Verse 42-43.
[11] The Holy Quran. Chapter 66 [The Prohibition; Arabic: *Al-Tahreem*]. Verse 11.

Prophet (s) relied on the support and backing of Khadija (a) to spread his message to the people.

Finally, Islam provides Lady Zahraa (a) as the best exemplar of excellence and perfection. She was the daughter of Prophet Muhammad (s) and Lady Khadija (a). Lady Fatima (a) was the greatest woman in the history of mankind. Even though the Holy Quran does not mention her name explicitly or directly, it does not mean that she is not in fact the greatest exemplar for us. The verses and narrations I mentioned previously, and there are others, are more than enough to support this well established fact. Lady Fatima (a) is one of the individuals of the Household (a) whom God described in the Quran, *"Indeed God desires to repel all impurity from you, O People of the Household, and purify you with a thorough purification."*[12]

She is the only woman that the Holy Prophet (s) brought forward with him when he was challenged by the Christians of Najran. The individuals that the Prophet (s) brought with him in accepting the challenge of the Christians of Najran was a clear sign of who represented the faith.

> *Should anyone argue with you concerning him, after the knowledge that has come to you, say, 'Come! Let us call our sons and your sons, our women and your women, our souls and your souls, then let us pray earnestly, and call down God's curse upon the liars.'*[13]

This event, which became known as *Al-Mubahala* (Debate), was a clear designation of Fatima (a) being the only woman

---

[12] The Holy Quran. Chapter 33 [The Parties; Arabic: *Al-Ahzab*]. Verse 33.
[13] The Holy Quran. Chapter 3 [Family of Imran; Arabic: *Aal Imran*]. Verse 61.

worthy of the status in those verses. 'Our sons' was embodied in the Prophet's grandsons, Hassan (a) and Hussain (a). 'Our souls' was embodied in the Prophet (s) himself and his cousin and son-in-law Ali (a). Finally, 'our women' was embodied in one person – Lady Fatima (a). The Messenger (s) only brought his daughter to represent that position and needed no one else. Lady Fatima (a) embodies this verse and the many others that discuss the Prophet (s) and his Household (a). As mentioned in the beginning of this chapter, she manifested the meaning of *Al-Kawthar* (the Abundance) in being the continuation of the message of Muhammad (s). She was the link between prophecy and guardianship – between the Prophet (s) and the Imams of the Progeny (a). The Messenger of God (s) has emphasized the truth of this continuation through his daughter, and that her children are essentially his children, in numerous narrations.[14]

LADY FATIMA (A) AS THE PERFECT EXEMPLAR

The four exemplars of excellence we previously mentioned each served humanity with their model of high ethics and morality. They surpassed other women and men in their excellence. The Grand Prophet (s) points to these women in that they are God's goodness gracing His Earth. It is narrated that Imam Moussa Al-Kadhim (a) said, *"The Messenger of God (s) said, 'God chose of women four: Mary, Asiyah, Khadija, and Fatima.'"*[15]

---

[14] Al-Majlisi, *Bihar Al-Anwar*, 43:228

[15] Ibid, 43:19

When we review each of their lives we realize that they each played a unique role. Mary (a), for example, was unique in her attainment of excellence through her specific acts of worship to God. The Holy Quran emphasizes her worship whereby she is frequently referenced in God's Book through her worship. *"O Mary, be obedient to your Lord and prostrate and bow down with those who bow [in worship]."*[16]

God also says, *"And Mary, daughter of Imran, who guarded the chastity of her womb, so We breathed into it of Our spirit. She confirmed the words of her Lord and His Books, and she was one of the obedient."*[17]

Asiyah was distinct in her champion-like stance of faith against her husband, the Pharaoh, as the Quran illustrates. She put everything on the line – wealth, security and status – and sacrificed all she had for the sake of her faith in God and the afterlife. The position she took with all the odds against her and the very fact that her husband was the tyrannical ruler of their civilization, let alone the era they lived in, deserves more than the attribute of awe-inspiring.

The same applied to the pure Lady Khadija (a) – the mother of Lady Fatima (a). She was unique in the tremendous role she played in her family. Her stances of solidarity and forbearance were unmatched. Her commitment to her faith in the message brought forth by the Messenger (s) was unrivalled. She gave everything for the sake of her faith and the divine mission of Islam. Her heart, mind, body and soul were wholly for Islam and its Prophet (s).

---

[16] The Holy Quran. Chapter 3 [Family of Imran; Arabic: *Aal Imran*]. Verse 43.
[17] The Holy Quran. Chapter 66 [The Prohibition; Arabic: *Al-Tahreem*]. Verse 12.

Lady Fatima (a) was 'crème de la crème' of these four immaculate women. She was not only the best lady of her time, but she was the best lady that ever set foot on this Earth. She was the manifestation of excellence and perfection. Fatima (a) was the highest exemplar of ethics, morality, justice, mercy and virtue. There are so many narrations of the Holy Prophet (s) describing the excellence and virtue of Fatima (a). In one narration he says,

> ... *It is as if when I look at my daughter Fatima (a) I have come to the Day of Judgment and am meeting a companion of light. To her right stand seventy thousand angels and to her left seventy thousand more. Before her hands are seventy thousand angels and behind her there are seventy thousand more. She leads the believing women of my nation into heaven. The woman that prayed her five prayers day and night, fasted the month of Ramadan, performed pilgrimage to the House of God, paid alms on her wealth, obeyed her husband, and gave allegiance to Ali (a) after me, will enter Paradise by the intercession of my daughter Fatima (a) – for she is the best of women of all time.*[18]

The reason for the distinction of Lady Fatima (a) goes back to her significance and the numerous roles she played in her short lifetime. The functions and responsibilities she held brought her to be the best woman humanity has witnessed and one of the few individuals that exemplify the complete human being. Below we will discuss some of the significant roles she played.

---

[18] Al-Majlisi, *Bihar Al-Anwar*, 43:24

THE ROLE OF LADY FATIMA (A) AS THE PERFECT HUMAN BEING

One of the most important elements of a person's life, and is in reality the purpose of one's life, is reaching God and knowing Him through one's pursuit for excellence in this life. Our very presence in this life is based on this essential concept. Perhaps of the most significant mechanisms in the pursuit for excellence are those of worship and knowledge. We highlight these two mechanisms in the life of Lady Fatima (a).

Worship

The Holy Quran discusses the importance of worship for the elevation and ascent of human beings toward their own perfection in a number of verses. God says, *"Though they were not commanded except to worship God, dedicating their faith to Him as men of pure faith, and to maintain the prayer and pay the zakat. That is the upright religion."*[19]

When Islam proposed the issue of worship, it did not mention it as something particular to men in opposed to women. Rather, in every aspect of worship it speaks to men and women together. When God says, *"O' those who believe"* that statement encompasses both men and women. Some verses go beyond that and actually speak to men and women individually, emphasizing that it is directed to both men and women. Take the following verse for example:

> *Indeed the muslim men and the muslim women, the faithful men and the faithful women, the obedient men and the*

---

[19] The Holy Quran. Chapter 98 [The Clear Proof; Arabic: *Al-Bayyinah*]. Verse 5.

*obedient women, the truthful men and the truthful women,
the patient men and the patient women, the humble men
and the humble women, the charitable men and the
charitable women, the men who fast and the women who
fast, the men who guard their private parts and the women
who guard, the men who remember God greatly and the
women who remember [God greatly]—God holds in store
for them forgiveness and a great reward.*[20]

This was purposed in establishing a new way of thinking –
that our excellence lies in worship – which applies to men
and women alike. Women equal men completely in this
aspect, for worship is not unique or reserved for men alone.
Even if there may be differences between men and women
in other aspects, there is no difference in this aspect. In
practice, God has given us these great examples of
immaculate women that reached the highest stage of human
excellence through their worship, like Mary (a) and Fatima
(a).

I wish to point to a one specific issue that will simplify the
significance that Lady Fatima (a) gave to worship – that is
Tasbeeh Al-Zahraa. This *tasbeeh*, or glorification, is one of the
greatest glorification prayers in our faith generating bounties
of award. It is narrated that Abi Abdillah (a) said, *"Tasbeeh
Al-Zahraa is from the frequent remembrance of God which He
described, 'O you who have faith! Remember God with frequent
remembrance.*[21],[22]

20 The Holy Quran. Chapter 33 [The Parties; Arabic: *Al-Ahzab*]. Verse 35.
21 The Holy Quran. Chapter 33 [The Parties; Arabic: *Al-Ahzab*]. Verse 41.
22 Al-Kulayni, *Al-Kafi*, 2:500.

He also said, *"Whoever glorified God using Tasbeeh Al-Zahraa before he moves from the position that concluded his prayer, God will forgive him before he begins with takbeer."*[23]

It is narrated that Imam Al-Sadiq (a) said to his companion, *"O' Aba Haroun, we instruct our children to do Tasbeeh Al-Zahraa just as we instruct them to uphold prayer..."*[24]

There are numerous other narrations like these. And the relevance here is that these narrations show the significance that Lady Fatima (a) attached to worship, that a specific form of glorification of God was named after her. She taught it to her children and they taught it to theirs – it became a ritual practice by Muslims near and far.

Prophet Muhammad (s) taught the glorification to Lady Fatima (a). Lady Fatima (a) was in need of some help with housework in her home. She wanted to ask her father about getting a maid but was bashful to make the request. He knew she was in need of something so he asked her what was wrong. Imam Ali (a) answered on her behalf and expressed that she needed a maid. The Prophet (s), able and willing to provide a maid for the house, told his daughter and son-in-law something else instead. He said, *"How about I teach you something that is better for you than a maid. After you conclude you prayer, say Allahu Akbar (God is Great) 34 times, Subhanallah (Glory be to God) 33 times, and Alhamdulillah (Praise be to God) 33 times."*[25] To this Lady Fatima (a) raised her head

---

[23] Al-Kulayni, *Al-Kafi*, 3:342.
[24] Al-Sadouq, *Thawab Al-A'mal*, 163.
[25] Al-Sadouq, *Men la Yahdarahu Al-Faqih*, 1:321.

and said, "*I am content with God and His Messenger... I am content with God and His Messenger.*"[26]

In another narration the Prophet (s) said, "*Subhanallah (Glory be to God) 33 times, Alhamdulillah (Praise be to God) 33 times, and Allahu Akbar (God is Great) 34 times.*"[27]

From these narrations we can see the deep connection between Lady Fatima (a) and her worship and remembrance of God. By the Prophet (s) merely presenting her with a specific way of glorifying God she was immediately content and saw much more value in it than the maid that she initially expressed a need for. This kind of contentment cannot be realized by a person who does not know the meaning of worship and enjoys it. Lady Fatima (a) did not ask for anything forbidden or looked down upon. Also, she was in a real need of assistance with house chores. In addition, the Prophet (s) was able and willing to provide her with a maid. With all that, she considered that small prayer of glorification that the Prophet (s) gifted her with to be greater and more valuable than if he were to give her a maid. Because of this incident so many Muslims receive the benefit and reward of reciting this glorification after their daily prayers in accordance to the prophetic tradition.

With this in mind, we should address an important issue that society faces on a general level. We generally look at women as having shortcomings, when in fact society has shortchanged women. When we discuss worship it seems as if it was ordained for men and not women. When we listen to stories from history we often hear about men that were

---

[26] Ibid.
[27] Al-Sadouq, '*Ilal Al-Shara'i*, 2:366.

able to achieve their human excellence through worship, whereas stories of women in this regard are rarely unmentioned. It is seriously wrong to think that night prayers are characteristic of men and not women. It is seriously wrong to think that supplication, glorification of God, visiting the shrines, and pilgrimage are all characteristic of men and not women.

We observe that to an extent there is much more opportunity and space given to men as opposed to women in shrines and places of worship. But women should have the full and equal right as men when it comes to access to worship, especially in such holy places. I do not condone the stereotypical brush stroke of absolute uniformity between men and women on all levels; however, at the very least on the level of worship women should take what is rightfully theirs.

Knowledge

Before discussing the knowledge aspect of Lady Fatima's (a) perfection, which composes the second foundation of her excellence, we should point to something that is essential to this conversation. Accepting what is said in a discussion is often contingent on the recipient's understanding of the person that is being spoken about. Thus, it is essential that to fully understand and benefit from these types of discussions that we do not place barriers between ourselves and the information that we receive from our narrations simply because they don't sound 'right' to us or that we are not 'convinced' by what is said.

When we receive any piece of information or knowledge about someone or something, the validity of that information falls on who the person or thing is. For example, if you were to tell your friend that Adam, who has absolutely no engineering or architectural experience and no external assistance, built a 300-floor skyscraper, would your friend believe you? Most definitely not, and they would be right not to because it does not reasonably follow that such a person would produce such a thing. However, if you told your friend that Gabriel, the world's top architectural engineer, was responsible for the construction of that skyscraper, wouldn't they believe you then? They would, because it is reasonable to expect such an excellent product from such an accomplished person. If your friend didn't believe you then, they are probably purposely being stubborn and inflexible.

This is often the case when some people react to some of the narrations. They jump to the conclusion that whatever is said is simply an exaggeration of the truth, merely because they are measuring the qualities, attributes, or conduct discussed in the narration against the abilities of regular people. Because the content does not reasonably apply to most people, the reader will deny it and feel justified in denying it. However, if the reader is to take a closer look and reflect to see that most of these narrations pertain to qualities and attributes unique to individuals that surpassed the masses. Narrations about Lady Fatima (a) are not anecdotes about any regular person or just another individual in the grander society of mankind. These are narrations pertaining to a woman whom the Prophet (s) described as being "a part of me." She is the individual that represents not only the continuation of the Messenger of

God's bloodline but also the extension of his immaculate spirit and divine ethics. She was the core of the holy household that God purified. She was the woman who the Imams of the Progeny (a) were proud to call 'our Mother'. Thus, when we read and learn about her qualities and attributes through the noble narrations, let us not be quick to dismiss the stories they hold.

The discussion of Lady Fatima's (a) knowledge is a lengthy one and cannot be encompassed by one chapter alone. Thus, I wish to focus on one particular aspect of her knowledge here – her arrival at the highest levels of knowledge and comprehension. The best evidence for this is her infallibility – she was immaculate in her thoughts, her creed, her conduct and demeanor. God honored her with purification for the flawless beam of light that she was. Infallibility is reliant on the foundations of knowledge and comprehension. The Infallibles are God's proof upon humanity, and an individual cannot be God's proof without having the foundations of knowledge and comprehension. One who is ignorant cannot be a representative of God to humanity, nor can one who is less knowledgeable be a proof or guide for those who are more knowledgeable. The fact that Lady Fatima (a) was infallible and, without a shadow of doubt, one of God's proofs, guides, and representatives on Earth speaks volumes to what knowledge, comprehension and wisdom she possessed.

It is enough that Imam Hassan Al-Askari, the 11th Imam of the Progeny, said, "*We [the Imams] are God's proof upon the Creation, and our mother Fatima (a) is God's proof upon us.*"[28] If

---

[28] Al-Mas'oudi, *Al-Asrar Al-Fatimiya*, 17.

Lady Fatima (a) was God's proof for the individuals that served as His proof and guide for all of creation, then what level of knowledge did she have? What secrets did she hold? The angels would speak to Fatima (a). They would frequent her home and seek blessings from the House of Prophecy. These angelic discussions were transcribed in what became known as the Psalms of Fatima (a), which were passed down from one Imam to the next. A number of narrations have mentioned and referenced these Psalms.

Hamad Ibn Uthman narrates that he heard Aba Abdillah (a) say, *"The deviants will appear in year 128, and that is because I looked at the Psalsm of Fatima (a)."* Hamad asked the Imam (a), "What is the Psalms of Fatima?" The Imam (a) replied,

> *When God's Prophet (s) returned to his Lord, a deep sorrow entered the heart of Fatima (a) – one that no one knows but God himself. So God sent her an angel to relieve her of her grief and speak to her. She told the Commander of the Faithful (a) about this, to which he said, 'When you have this feeling and you hear that voice tell me.' She did exactly that. The Commander of the Faithful (a) would write everything he heard turning his pages into a book. There is nothing in it pertaining to the laws of what is permissible and what is forbidden; in it, however, is the knowledge of what will be.*[29]

Without delving into the detailed depths of this narration, there are generally a few points to make note of here:

1) The issue of angels speaking to human beings is something that the Holy Quran discusses in a

---

[29] Al-Kulayni, *Al-Kafi*, 1:240.

number of places. There are several women in the Quran that were spoken to by angels. Take the examples of Mary (a), The mother of Moses (a), and Abraham's (a) wife. So it is not far-fetched that the greatest of all women would speak to the angels.

2) There is a false accusation against the followers of the Progeny (a) that they have an alternative Quran called "The Psalms of Fatima."[30] This is a blatant lie. No one claims that the Psalms of Fatima is a divine book of revelation. A number of narrations clearly state that there are no elements of the Quran in the Psalms; rather, it is a book that contains knowledge of the future – and it is only held in the hands of the Imams of the Progeny (a).

3) Reaching this status whereby she is receiving knowledge by divine teaching, means that she has the true knowledge of reality. It is one thing to learn by means of observation and acquiring information, it is another to attain knowledge from God. That knowledge cannot be compared to any other, because it is not prone to error nor can it have the possibility of mistake. It is the knowledge of the reality of things not simply a perception of what is apparent.

From these two fundamental elements – worship and knowledge – Lady Fatima (a) was able to, with the grace of God, to manifest human perfection in the best way. She was able to realize the highest levels of this perfection. She

---

[30] In Arabic, *Mushaf Fatima (a)*.

became the epicenter of infallibility and purity, and the nexus between prophecy and guardianship.

HER ROLE WITH FAMILY AND THE HOME

With all the unique qualities Lady Fatima (a) had, she refused to live a life that was filled with luxury and comfort. After all, she was:

1) The closes to the heart of her father Muhammad (s). She was orphaned of her mother as Lady Khadija (a) passed away when Fatima (a) was only a little girl. Prophet Muhammad (s) naturally filled this void with his extra care and attention to Fatima (a).

2) Lady Fatima (a) married at a young age and thus took on the responsibilities of wife, and mother, early on and met the challenges of these roles.

3) She was the daughter of the greatest man of the age, let alone of all ages. Given that he was the leader of his people he had so many social responsibilities, which Fatima (a) helped him with often. So naturally because of these factors she would not be expected to take care of what traditional housewives and stay-at-home mothers would. Maids and domestic workers could have easily been employed to assume the responsibilities of the home.

We find that this was absolutely not the case, however. With all of the challenges and responsibilities, Lady Fatima (a) used to assume all the responsibilities of her household even though she was fatigued and exhausted given the rest of her roles and obligations.

Consider the narration that was mentioned previously in the chapter, when Lady Fatima (a) was in need of a maid. Fatima (a) would sweep, mop, prepare food, cook, clean, and more until her body would ache. And when her father gifted her with the glorification that became known as *Tasbeeh Al-Zahraa* instead of a maid, she was more than content. There are few things to take away from this, some of which include:

A Simple Life

When we follow the life of the Prophet (s) and his family we note that they lived a very simple life. The Muslims in general, with the exception of only some, were mostly impoverished. In addition, the Prophet (s) focused on spreading the divine message of God and thus exerted his efforts in helping people and manifesting his purpose as the Mercy to Mankind. So his family followed his example and endured much hardship so that others would not be disenfranchised by their own challenges. Muhammad (s) was the Prophet of God, the leader of a nation, and head of a state and yet lived a life simpler than most of his followers – he was the best example and role model for all.

Guidance

The Progeny (a) are the most knowledgeable people of the reality of this world and its value with God. Therefore, they did not give much importance to the superficial material things in life. What was more important to them was delivering the divine message of God, guiding people to Him, and actualizing the will of God on Earth. The 'finer' things in life did not attract them, nor did it distract them for one moment from their primary goal being the development of humanity. This development towards excellence could only be realized with the right role models and examples for people to follow. The Progeny (a) played that very role.

Jabir Al-Ansari narrates that the Prophet (s) saw Fatima (a) clothed in a coarse blanket, toiling as she grinded grain, and nursing her child at the same time. His eyes filled with tears, the Prophet (s) said to Fatima (a), "My daughter, rush toward the bitterness of this world [so that you may attain] the sweetness of the hereafter." To that she replied, "O' Messenger of God, praise be to God for his blessings, and thanks be to God for his favors."[31] The narration states that at that moment God revealed the following verse to the Holy Prophet (s), *"Soon your Lord will give you [that with which] you will be pleased."*[32]

Balance

Lady Fatima (a), being the greater teacher by example that she was, shows us the importance of balancing responsibilities, remaining humble, and having forbearance and patience. She showed us that taking care of the household is an honor and a blessing. Thus, it would be a grave mistake for us to assume, men and women alike, that for a woman to dedicate her time and effort in taking care of her home would be some form of disgrace to her. Lady Fatima (a) displayed to us through the work of her own honorable hands the significance of caring for the home and the sanctity that is reserved in doing so. Our narrations

---

31 Al-Majlisi, Bihar Al-Anwar, 43: 86
32 The Holy Quran. Chapter 33 [The Parties; Arabic: *Al-Ahzab*]. Verse 41.

emphasize this truth and honor this role of the woman in the household as a form of *jihad* (struggle), which could be one of the reasons for being rewarded with Paradise. It is narrated from Imam Al-Sadiq (a) that Um Salama asked the Messenger of God (s) about the reward of women in this regard. To that he said, *"Whenever a woman [does anything in the home no matter how minor] with the intent of doing good, God will look at her [with favor]. Whoever God looks at [with favor] will not be punished."*[33]

What is even more inspiring is that when Lady Fatima (a) did get a maid – Fidda – she would split the housework with her maid. Lady Fatima (a) never got rid of her work clothes because she continued to work in her home even with the presence of a maid.

And thus, we continue to emphasize with our dear daughters and our respected sisters the importance of this responsibility. A woman is the most able and apt to assume and fulfill the responsibility of ensuring a solid home is built for a family to grow and be nurtured. If the greatest woman that walked this Earth carried this responsibility with pride, does it not follow that our daughters and sisters should do the same? If it were not so important Lady Fatima (a) would not have done it.

Family

This was a role that was unique to Lady Fatima (a) when compared to the other great examples of women in history. Lady Mary (a) did not have a family whereby she was responsible for the administration of a household. Her life

---

[33] Al-Tousi, *Al-Amali*, 618

solely revolved around her worship. In addition, her son Jesus (a) was not like the regular young boys in need of the constant attention of a mother; thus, Mary (a) did not have the trial of practicing this domestic role. In regards to Lady Asiyah and Lady Khadija (a) I will mention the words of some of our venerated scholars.

> *For Asiyah, the wife of Pharaoh, her circumstances were not conducive to having a complete family. Though she was married, she did not have any children. In addition, her husband was an oppressive tyrant; thus, she was not able to exercise and promote the ethics and morals characteristic of a strong family unit. On the other hand, Lady Khadija (a) had a significant role from the aspect of family and household. For she was the wife of the Messenger of God (s) and the mother of his Progeny (a). Lady Fatima (a), however, was unique even when compared to her mother due to the various roles she played in her life.[34]*

HER ROLE IN PUBLIC LIFE

Generally, women were not seen to have much significance in most societies in history. Thus, it was not acceptable for women to voice out their opinions in public discourse and engage in civic society. Indeed, in the history of the Arabians and in other past societies there were women that played significant roles in public life and even sat at the helm of power. Examples include Balqees the Queen of Sheba and Zenobia the Queen of Palmyra. Excluding these exceptions, society did not look at women as being worthy

---

[34] Al-Hakeem, *Al-Zahraa: Sermons and Discussions of Shaheed Al-Mihrab Ayatullah Sayyid Muhammad Baqir Al-Hakeem*, 213 .

to express opinions or be involved in the public sphere. Islam rejected this condescending and backwards mentality. The faith promoted a view that empowered women so much so that it presented an example of a woman who can attain the highest status known to man – the status of guardianship, which was embodied in Lady Fatima (a). God says,

> *But the faithful, men and women, are comrades of one another: they bid what is right and forbid what is wrong and maintain the prayer, give the zakat, and obey God and His Apostle. It is they to whom God will soon grant His mercy. Indeed God is all-mighty, all-wise.*[35]

Included in the greater message of the Holy Prophet (s) is the enfranchisement of women and giving them their due rights. This was not reserved to the abstract theoretical declarations; it was through the practical implementation, which Lady Fatima (a) worked to manifest. The following are examples of these efforts from her life.

Teacher

Lady Fatima (a) was a scholar and educator in her own right. She regularly taught members of the community, women and men according to some narrations. She was the model for excellence that Muslim women sought out for their own development and advancement. Our narrations detail and praise her accomplishments in this regard.

---

[35] The Holy Quran. Chapter 9 [The Repentance; Arabic: *Al-Tawba*]. Verse 71.

Leader

The daughter of the Messenger (s) was very keen to social interaction and responsibility. She would make sure to attend social functions that took place in Medina. The fact that she was the Lady of Light, the daughter of the Prophet (s), the wife of the Commander of the Faithful (a), should be taken into consideration in this regard as well. When she attended somewhere it was just any other member of the community attending. Nonetheless, she never made others feel that way. She carried herself humbly and simply, as a mercy and blessing to those in her midst.

She also cared dearly for the poor and the weak. Her home was always full of the less fortunate. Even when she was exhausted and spread so thin, her home still embraced all these people and her blessings continued to encompass them all. Her home was their safe haven. Not one person ever left the house of Fatima (a) disappointed. It is enough to have the Holy Quran as testimony to her sacrifices in the three consecutive days of giving all the food she had to the poor, the orphan, and the prisoner. *"For the love of Him, they feed the needy, the orphan and the prisoner."*[36] Lady Fatima gave her food, the newest of her clothes, and practically anything she had of worth to help people in need.

The care and attention that Lady Fatima (a) gave to her neighbors was above and beyond. She not only cared for her neighbors publically but privately as well. She would constantly pray for her neighbors before she even prayed for herself. It is narrated that Imam Hassan (a) said,

---

[36] The Holy Quran. Chapter 76 [Man; Arabic: *Al-Insaan*]. Verse 8.

I saw my mother Fatima (a) praying on the eve of Friday.
She continued to kneel and prostrate until sunrise. I heard
her pray for the believing men and women, each by his or
her name. She would pray for them so much and not
mention herself in her prayer at all. [Later] I asked her,
'Mother, why don't you pray for yourself the way you pray
for others?' She replied, 'My son, your neighbor then your
home.'[37]

If this points to anything, it points to the fact that Lady
Fatima (a) was so caring and selfless that she thought of
others before she thought of herself. You cannot have such
an honorable spirit without really caring and feeling
responsibility for others. Let's take a simple lesson her from
her beautiful example. Caring for others doesn't necessarily
have to be in material means, it could be as simple as
praying for another person, which can have tremendous
effects. It is from here we can see that Islam has
emphasized the importance of praying for others.

Hero

Lady Fatima (a) was present in a number of important yet
dangerous situations. Our narrations state that she
participated in some of the battles of the Prophet (s). Along
with other women, she assisted in caring for the wounded
soldiers of the battlefield. One of the practical pieces of
evidence that clearly support this is the construction of a
mosque in the honor of Lady Fatima (a) at the site of the
battle of Khandaq. There are a number of mosques that
were built in the honor of the Prophet (s) and some

---

[37] Al-Sadouq, *'Ilal Al-Shara'i*, 1:182

companions in the places that they prayed while breaking from the battlefield – some of which are still standing today. The Mosque of Fatima (a) at Khandaq is a testament to Fatima's (a) presence at the battle of Khandaq. Though the narrations do not specify the exact role she played and the practices she utilized, her mere presence is evidence for her participation and importance in this regard.

Supporter

The most important role that Lady Fatima (a) played was her steadfast stance beside the Commander of the Faithful (a) against those who oppressed him. That discussion requires much detail and time. What I wish to point to is the significance of Fatima's (a) stance in the greater scheme of things. After individuals ascended to power and bypassed the authority of Imam Ali (a) in succeeding the Holy Prophet (s), Imam Ali (a) was not able to demand for his rights in a substantial way. He had little supporters and was accused of having the desire to rule over the rest of the Muslims. Lady Fatima (a) came forward to defend Imam Ali (a) not simply as her husband, but as her Imam and the rightful successor to the Messenger of God. Her stance was not out of greed or desire for power that was lost. Worldly status and power had no value to her. The Prophet (s) told her that she would be the first to follow him after his death, so she knew the risk that was associated in standing for justice. She lived and endured through trials and tribulations, it was characteristic of her to stand for the truth. In essence, there was no other person qualified to make the stance that Lady Fatima (a) made and it was not possible for anyone else to take that position but her. Thus, she sacrificed her own life for the sake of this principle and defiantly stood against the oppressors. To her last breath, she continued to stand for the principle of true guardianship after the Holy Prophet (s).

CONCLUSION

This discussion sheds light on the greatness of Lady Fatima (a) through the various roles that she assumed. This greatness was not realized simply by practice, but it was her ability to completely fulfill all of these roles in the most perfect way. She was able to manifest perfection in balancing between her excellence in worship, knowledge and comprehension and her role as a mother, wife, scholar, teacher, and active participant leader in her society and community.

We ask God to give us the blessing of benefiting from Lady Fatima (a) by taking from the lessons of her life. We ask him to allow us to be from her followers and lovers and resurrect us as such on the Day of Judgment.

BIOGRAPHICAL INFORMATION

Name: Fatima

Title: Al-Zahraa

Kunya (Agnomen): Ummu'l-A'immah.

Father: Prophet Muhammad

Mother: Khadijah bint Khuwaylid

Born: Friday, 20th Jumadil-Thani in the fifth year after the declaration of the Prophethood (615 AD)

Birthplace: Mecca

Died: 14th of Jumadil-Awwal 11 AH (632 AD)

Place of Death: Medina

Age at Death: 18

Gravesite: Jannatul-Baqi', Medina, Saudi Arabia

IMAM HASSAN
The Flower of the Prophet's (s) Heart

In the Name of God, the most Beneficent, the most Merciful

It is narrated that Lady Fatima (a) came to her father Muhammad (s) with her young sons Hassan (a) and Hussain (a). *"O' Messenger of God, these are your sons so [what do you] bequeath to them,"* Fatima (a) said to her father. The Prophet (s) replied, *"Hassan will have my prestige and my status, while Hussain will have my bravery and generosity."*[1]

Imam Hassan (a) lived oppressed and died oppressed. This of course is not foreign to the Household of Prophecy. God blessed the people with their presence, but they did not know the value and worth of the gems that lived amongst them. The people went farther than lack of appreciation and value to oppress and strip their rights from them. They were so fervent in oppressing the Prophet's (s) progeny it was as if the Prophet (a) had commanded them to do so. It was as if the Quran did not clearly state the obligation in loving

---

[1] Ibn Al-Atheer, *Usud Al-Ghaba*, 5:467

and caring or the Prophet's (s) family. God says, "*Say, 'I do not ask you any reward for it except the love of [my] relatives.*"[2]

Though the entire Progeny (a) was oppressed, Imam Hussain (a) was unique in how he was oppressed. The Imam (a) was oppressed by not only his enemies, but by his followers and supporters as well. When a person is oppressed, the pain of oppression can be eased knowing that you have a group around you that shares in your pain and stands by you. Imam Hassan (a), however, did not have that benefit. He was oppressed during his lifetime and even after his martyrdom, by both his enemies and his followers. Many of his followers did not understand the latent meaning and purpose behind his movement and the decisions that he made. They didn't realize that what he did saved Islam and the lives of so many Muslims. His decisions laid the foregrounds for the greatest renaissances in the history of Islam, let alone the history of humanity – the renaissance, revolution, and movement of his brother Imam Hussain (a).

In this chapter, I do not wish to delve into the discussion of Imam Hassan's (a) peace accord with Muawiya, which most people even to this day do not understand. Imam Hassan (a) was subjected to a massive propaganda campaign initiated by the Umayyads to defame his personality and ruin his name. Muawiya invested a huge amount of capital into this campaign, paying people to spread false accusations against Imam Hassan (a) by the pulpit, pen and word of mouth. The greater tragedy is that most people believed it and continue to hold these false conceptions of Imam Hassan

---

[2] The Holy Quran. Chapter 42 [The Consultation; Arabic: *Al-Shoura*]. Verse 23.

(a) to this very day. It is as if we do not have minds to process, assess, and scrutinize the information we receive. It is as if logic is so foreign to us that anything we hear on the radio, or watch on television, or read in books of history must be absolutely correct.

Some historians participated in this heinous crime of defaming Imam Hassan (a). By not sharing the correct and full picture of what actually took place so many years ago, they continue to reinforce the slander and defamation that was activated by the enemies of the Prophet's (s) family. Why did these historians take part in this? These are some reasons:

1) They personally believe what they have written and the images portrayed coincide with their beliefs. Thus, they do not feel the need to delve deeper or scrutinize their findings because it works well with their creed and worldview, or

2) They were after the payouts that the Umayyads readily provided to any man that was willing to carry a pen and transcribe the propaganda into books that would later on be references for history. Muawiya was fixed on tainting the image of Imam Hassan (a) and his family, fully capable and willing to buy people's loyalty and conscience – all for the right price. That is what he did and that is what some "historians" allowed themselves to be subject to. Or,

3) They were hesitant to write the truth and describe the events as they actually occurred out of fear of

the wrath of the caliphs. History is often written by those in power.

And thus, what was written of history was dictated by such reasons crafting an image of individuals in people's mind that is so far from the truth. To this day many of our people still suffer from the repercussions of the Umayyads' smear campaigns. Given that we live in the "age of information" – as we like to call it – we must reassess our reading of history regarding two fundamental issues:

A. Knowing the truth and doing justice to those that were oppressed in history. This issue deserves our time and effort. Supporting those who are oppressed does not stop at the sword and fighting in battle, we are capable of supporting justice through our pens. This should be especially utilized given the freedom we have in many of our societies to express ourselves and advocate justice through our writing, without the fear of punishment by the regime of caliphs that existed in our history.

B. It is within the tradition of life for nations to build their culture and society based on their history. In other words, of the most important mechanisms for the success of a society is that it is established with its nation's history in mind. If its history is fabricated or false then without a doubt some aspects of that foundation will not be sound. Thus, without a sound foundation such a society will be unable to stay intact and move forward in the correct way, because heritage and history have instrumental significance in providing the foundation for a sound, strong, formidable society to grow and flourish. With a fabricated heritage the foundation is susceptible to corruption and ruin.

Perhaps one of the reasons for our regression within the greater construct of civilizations – when we were previously the nation that God chose to be a witness for the rest of nations, *"Thus We have made you a middle nation that you may be witnesses to the people,"*[3] – is that we have latched on to much of what we have inherited in false history without scrutinizing what we have received. We find ourselves in a blunder between many of the events that took place and are confused between what is 'Islamic Thought' and what was practiced by the Umayyads and the Abbasids. In other words, we are unable to find harmony between what is theory and what was actually practiced. It is astounding how we find some analysts of history try to reconcile between the ideological reality of the Islamic community and the historical reality that existed. Very little actually go forth to scrutinize the accounts of history that exist of which have so many flaws, errors, and fabrications.

Today, we are most in need of studying our history and applying it to the scrutiny of logic and analytical reasoning. We need to accept what is logical within it and reject what is not reasonably sound. Such a task is not simple or easy and it becomes more and more difficult to correct past mistakes as time passes.

Pertaining to Imam Hassan (a), he is the individual that the Prophet (s) described as with love, respect and endearment.

---

[3] The Holy Quran. Chapter 2 [The Cow; Arabic: *Al-Baqara*]. Verse 143.

He described him as his beloved grandson, a leader, a master, a man of nobility, and the 'leader of the youth of paradise' along with his brother Hussain (a). With all that the Prophet (s) described him with – and the Prophet (s) does not speak out of his own whim for he is nothing but revelation – these attributes were of no mention by those audacious historians. They painted Imam Hassan (a) as a personality who had no aim or purpose but to fulfill his carnal desires, to spend wealth extravagantly, and to accept money and gifts from Muawiya to further feed his extravagant pursuits. I really don't know how these people will stand before God on the Day of Judgment with their grave sin of tarnishing the image of Imam Hassan (a) – an individual so pure that the Prophet (s) praised whenever he was in the Prophet's (s) presence.

I wish to briefly discuss some of these misconceptions and clarify a few significant points.

IMAM HASSAN (A) AS A PACIFIST

Some have portrayed Imam Hassan (a) as a weak personality who was unwilling to fight or resist and thus stepped down from the seat of the caliphate. Others have tried to explain that Imam Hassan (a) was rather a more peaceful personality that did not wish to shed blood. In other words, they claimed he was a pacifist. But in that explanation they are essentially doing injustice to Imam Ali (a) and Imam Hussain (a). Were Imam Ali (a) and Imam Hussain (a) not peaceful? Were they content with shedding blood while Imam Hassan (a) didn't? To the people that bring forth this notion of Imam Hassan (a), did you read the history of the wars and battles Imam Hassan (a) not only participated in but was at the forefront defending the honor of Islam? Did you not read about the bravery and valor of this Imam (a) who never fell short from defending Islam and his father the Commander of the Faithful (a). Imam Hassan (a) and Imam Hussain (a) would lunge toward the forefront of every battle and bring themselves to the heart of combat, leading their fellow warriors with a faith, conviction, and trust in God that was unmatched.

Imam Hassan (a) was not a pacifist as some have mistakenly concluded. Especially when compared to Imam Ali (a) and Imam Hussain (a), there is no difference between Imam Hassan (a) and his father and brother. He is of them and like them completely. He was not happy with not going to war with Muawiya and stepping down from the caliphate. People have mistakenly concluded that the Imam (a) was more willing to not go to war and avoid bloodshed than keeping the caliphate and establishing a just government like his father's. What is even worse is that people, to this day, still do not differentiate between the truce with Muawiya and abdication of the divine religious authority that succeeded the Prophet (s) onto Imam Ali (a) and then onto Imam Hassan (a).

This again is a lengthy discussion in itself, but in summary I will say that Imam Hassan (a) struck the peace accord with Muawiya due to the dire circumstances that surrounded him. The peace accord was the only way he could protect the Progeny (a) of the Prophet (s) and the companions of the Commander of the Faithful (a). What he did laid the grounds for Imam Hussain (a) to execute his movement of revolution and reform. Imam Hassan (a) endured beyond what we can comprehend, just like his grandfather the Messenger of God (s) endured. I would draw an insightful parallel between the controversy of Imam Hassan's (a) accord with Muawiya and the Muslims' misconception of the Prophet's (s) Hudaybiya Accord.

TAKING MONEY FROM MUAWIYA

There has been a floating accusation against Imam Hassan (a) that he accepted money and gifts from Muawiya to spend on his wives and harems. These notions come forth from charged fabricated narrations. We do not deny that some narrations that point to Imam Hassan (a) accepting money from Muawiya do exist. But before we delve into the debate of this issue, it would be beneficial to point to other narrations that say that Imam Hassan (a) would reject Muawiya's money and overtures. This is in addition to the fact that Imam Hassan (a) was far from being a poor or needy person. When Imam Ali (a) was not in governance, he owned swaths of land. Imam Hassan (a) and Imam Hussain (a) managed much of the land, which produced bounties of crops that brought in a lot of revenue. Imam Hassan (a) in particular was characteristic of spending much of the money he earned on the poor and needy. He became known as the 'Generous of the Progeny'. Thus, he was clearly in no need for money gifts from anyone, let alone Muawiya.

Nonetheless, if we were to entertain these narrations that say he did take money gifts from Muawiya, there are a number of points to consider:

First, given that Imam Hassan (a) is an infallible it would follow that we accept his actions and give him the benefit of the doubt. Even though we don't know the details of these occurances or we might be tempted to reject them at first sight.[4]

Second, the money at issue is in the hands of a tyrannical ruler. It is well established in Islamic law that there is no wrong done in taking that money. Sayyid Al-Murtada says,

> *Taking overtures is permissible, and even mandatory. This is because all the money that is in the hands of a tyrant ruling over the nation must be taken by the Imam and the Muslims in whatever way possible and placed in its appropriate places. If he was not able to take back all the money, which is the property of God, from the hands of Muawiya, but was able to take some by means of overture it is mandatory for him to take it and distribute it rightfully. Because discretion with this money is only the right of the vicegerent, which was only existent in the person of Imam Hassan (a) at the time. No one can rightfully say that the overtures he accepted from Muawiya were spent on himself or his family. That money was only used in its legal and appropriate place, for even his own money he would spend it on the poor and less fortunate.[5]*

Moreover, Imam Hassan (a) most definitely did not spend such money on himself or his families as others have depicted. He was responsible for scores of families that lost their loved ones in battle alongside Imam Ali (a) in the battles of *Jamal, Siffin,* and *Nahrawan.*

---

[4] Al-Murtada, *Tanzeeh Al-Anbiya'*, 221.

[5] Ibid, 225.

Finally, taking money from one who has control over the treasury is not something shameful, even if the one in control is a tyrant. That money is the right of the Muslims and is their money in essence. Imam Hassan (a) was the leader of the Muslims, and thus he has more right over that money than anyone else. Thus, if Muawiya were to send money to Imam Hassan (a) it would not be a gift, it would be the actual ordained right of the Imam (a).

REGARDING THE WIVES OF IMAM HASSAN (A)

A number of history books, unfortunately, have tried to depict Imam Hassan (a) as an individual who married and divorced so frequently that it appeared as if marriage was a hobby or game for him. They tried to position him as having no aspiration or worry other than to marry and divorce. They argue that because of his sole desire to marry and divorce repeatedly, to fulfill his carnal desires, he stepped down from the caliphate to free himself for his personal romantic life. Some historical narrations say that he married up to 70 women and others mention the fantastical number of 300 women. Without even addressing these laughable figures, we know for certain that these books and narrations have tried to paint a loathsome picture of Imam Hassan (a). To refute these false accusations and despicable claims, there are a few points to bear in mind:

1) There is no doubt that the Umayyad hand has its place in the lies and fabrications of these issues. It is unfathomable to combine this accusations with the personality and character that Imam Hassan (a) possessed. With so many narrations by the Holy

Prophet (s) and the Commander of the Faithful (a) about the status, nobility, honor and merit of Imam Hassan (a) we stand bewildered at how anyone could accept or even entertain such appalling claims against the grandson of the Holy Prophet (s).

2) Imam Hassan (a) was an individual who was tasked with great responsibilities at the time of his father Ali (a). It is not reasonable to presume that someone with so many social responsibilities and with a schedule full of duties and obligations toward people would be engaged in such unnatural habits. In addition, wouldn't Imam Ali (a) have noticed his son's lifestyle and prevent him from engaging in such behavior? After all, he belonged to the household of the Commander of the Faithful (a), which was by default a family that was immersed in public life by mere virtue of who they were. Wouldn't Imam Ali (a) have prevented his son from these things that would insult his home and would have caused so many problems with so many families given that his son was supposedly divorcing all of their daughters and marrying others?

3) If we were to continue to entertain the notion that Imam Hassan (a) was actually one who married frequently, there is a peculiar irregularity in the accounts of history. If he had 70 or even 300 wives, then why don't these historical accounts mention more than the names of five women? Because whatever numbers have been added beyond those names are simply figments of the historian's imagination. Moreover, historians – such as Al-

Shaykh Al-Mufeed – do not mention Imam Hassan (a) having more than 15 children, male and female. If he dozens, let alone hundreds, of wives like some of these laughable narrations mention we would think that the he would have more than 15 children.

4) Those who accuse Imam Hassan (a) of marrying and divorcing so much have failed to mention all the women that he actually divorced. Even the historians that make such a claim have not been able to provide proof for this. They have only named two women of the claimed divorcees. The first was a woman from the tribe of *Bani Sheban* who adopted the beliefs of the *Kharajites*, who waged war on the Commander of the Faithful in the Battle of *Nahrawan*. The second woman was Hafsa or Hind bint Abdelrahman ibn Abu Bakr. So how did he marry and divorce all these dozens and hundreds of women while narrations only mention these two names. Where are the rest of the claimed divorcees?

THE ACCORD OF AL-HASSAN (A)

It is narrated that the Messenger of God (s) said, *"Hassan and Hussain are Imams, whether they rise or settle."*[6]

Like his younger brother Hussain (a), Imam Hassan (a) was a victim of oppression and heavy tribulations. The oppression against Imam Hassan (a) was unique in that so many have misunderstood him and the role he played in saving Islam and its divine message. To many Muslims,

---

[6] Al-Ahsa'i, *'Awali Al-La'ali*, 4:93.

including followers of the Progeny (a), Imam Hassan (a) was passive and unwilling to continue the legacy of just governance that his father Ali (a) established. The greater injustice done is when people compare between Imam Hassan (a) and Imam Hussain (a), suggesting that Imam Hussain (a) was the better of the two.

Such a senseless comparison does injustice to both of our Imams (a), because of the implicit stab that it takes at the entire system of *imamah*. Who are we to make such a comparison and evaluate what stance by which imam was better? Divine guardianship through the actions and decisions of the vicegerents is not a trivial matter that can be toyed with by people who wish to make shallow comparisons and contrasts. God says,

> *A faithful man or woman may not have any option in their matter, when God and His Apostle have decided on a matter, and whoever disobeys God and His Apostle has certainly strayed into manifest error.*[7]

The general authority of the Holy Prophet (s) succeeded to the immaculate Imams (a). Thus, defiance of the Imam (a) is defiance of the Prophet (s), and defiance of the Prophet (s) is defiance of God. You cannot enjoy the attribute of faith without accepting this and falling in line with the authority of God, His Prophet (s), and His vicegerents. The Holy Prophet (s) emphasized the authority of Imam Hassan (a) and Imam Hussain (a) in every matter, situation, and condition. Whether they settle or rise, whether they speak or remain silent, they are the authority over the believers and

---

[7] The Holy Quran. Chapter 32 [The Parties; Arabic: *Al-Ahzab*]. Verse 36.

the representatives of God on Earth after the Prophet (s). Therefore, there is no meaning in giving merit to one stance over the other, as in preferring Imam Hussain's (a) rise versus Imam Hassan's (a) accord. Because, in essence, each of the Imams would have done the same thing that the other did considering their situation and circumstances. So long as the decision is made by the Immaculate then there is no permissibility in expressing one's opinions in the matter or to attempt to wrong the Imam's decision. Such insolence would be outside the scope of faith.

It is important to realize the significance of Imam Hassan's (a) stance and its role in protecting the religion and actually preparing the foregrounds for the revolution of Imam Hussain (a). They are together in essence the same movement and the same decision. The silence of Hassan (a) is the silence of Hussain (a) and the rise of Hussain (a) is the rise of Hassan (a). In other words, Imam Hassan's (a) accord with Muawiya was *Hussaini* and Imam Hussain's (a) revolution was *Hassani*.

CIRCUMSTANCES

When we understand the circumstances that Imam Hassan (a) lived in we can understand the divine wisdom of the Imam and the position that he took.

Popular Base

Looking back at the popular base that was needed to fight Muawiya, we find that there was a grave lacking in loyalty. Though Kufa was full of loyalists and followers of Imam Ali

(a) at his time, there were also significant numbers of other groups like the following:

The Kharajites. They were not a small group, but even as a minority they caused a lot of havoc. They made it a priority to instigate against the Imams (a) and openly challenge their positions. Their goal was to continue escalating the conflict with Muawiya no matter what the circumstances. They told Imam Hassan (a) that their paying of allegiance to him was contingent on this matter. He refused to accept such an allegiance. Audaciously, they went to Imam Hussain (a) and told him that they would pay allegiance to him instead. Imam Hussain (a) dismissed them and stated firmly that he would never take allegiance from them so long as Al-Hassan was alive. Interestingly enough these Kharajites, who were so bent on fighting Muawiya, worked with the Umayyads against Imam Hassan (a) and Imam Hussain (a).[8]

The Sellouts. There is a significant number of people who should not be dismissed so easily, and those are 'the sellouts'. These people did not care about principle or faith, they jumped on any opportunity to bring them money or power. It didn't matter who would be sacrificed, as long as they were on the winning side. This group of people are extremely dangerous because at any moment they will sell the people around them for the right price.

Gangs and Tribes. This group is also significant because most of them did not act based on principle or faith either. Whatever the chief of their tribe or the head of their gang said, they followed.

---

[8] Al-Adeeb, *Al-A'imma Al-Ithna 'Ashr*, 94.

Umayyad Emissaries. These people played the role of propaganda, leading the way in the psychological war on the people. They caused doubt and stirred instigation against Imam Hassan (a). Some were caught and punished, others continued in corruption and sedition.

Imam Hassan (a) was not able to rely on a solid base that was absolutely loyal to him. The Muslim community, especially during the time of the Commander of the Faithful (a), divided into numerous groups whereby many different opinions manifested – the Kharajites, the sellouts, and Muawiya who was characteristic of causing instigation, sedition, and civil unrest. All of this weakened the popular base and made it unfit for the Imam (a) to rely on. This is especially coupled with the fact that Imam Hassan (a) did not employ the same tactics of bribery, blackmail, and payouts like Muawiya did. The goal of the Imam Hassan (a), as was the goal of the Imams of the Progeny (a) collectively, was the developing individuals and communities of excellence. He had no interest in buying people's loyalty, he was more interested in investing in people's personal growth and development by emphasizing principle and ethics.

Psychological Readiness

At the time of Imam Hassan (a) people did not have the spirit or stomach for war anymore. Especially after so many battles that were waged on the caliphate of Imam Ali (a), people were exhausted and morale was low. This is in addition to the consistent resolute policies and firm politics of principle that Imam Ali (a) vindicated. Many were tired of it. They didn't see the vision and were frustrated with the short-term. Imam Ali's (a) sole concern was building a strong moral society without employing any of devious tactics like bribery, blackmail, treachery or betrayal. Some of his companions suggested that he send money to the chiefs of some of the tribes to buy back their loyalty, after Muawiya bought many of them out. They specifically proposed to take the money that was being given to the non-Arabs and the poor, and instead give it to the nobles of Quraysh and other Arab tribes. To that Imam Ali (a) replied,

> *You ask me to request victory through tyranny? No, by God, I will not so long as the sun rises and the stars shine in the sky. By God, if the money [of the treasury] was mine I would still disperse it amongst them [the non-Arabs and the poor]. So how would you ask me to do otherwise when the money [of the treasury] is theirs?[9]*

All of this led to immorality, decadence, and lethargy, making many unwilling to go to war. This was clear when the Imam (a) called for battle as the people responded lethargically and showed little will to support the cause. In battle, this lack of will and weak morale substantially weakens the ranks of a military and cannot be relied on to guarantee victory.

Concealing the Truth

After the martyrdom of the Commander of the Faithful (a) and his appointment of Imam Hassan (a) to succeed him, the atmosphere was full of misconceptions and doubts regarding leadership. Soured by war and easily swayed by

---

[9] Al-Majlisi, *Bihar Al-Anwar*, 93:164.

the propanda of the Umayyads, many thought that the conflict between Imam Hassan (a) and Muawiya was simply a dispute between two families. These people had no conviction in the principle of imamah, though it is found in all of our primary religious texts. And though Imam Hassan (a) was the divinely appointment imam of the people, much of the masses became accustomed to unfounded methods of discerning leadership. What was known as *shura* – a system where a leader was chosen by the aristocracy, giving a false sense of legitimacy – became a norm of practice, straying away from the foundational principles of guardianship by divine appointment. Thus, people mistakenly thought that the conflict that existed between Muawiya and Imam Ali (a), followed by Imam Hassan (a), was simply two prominent families competing. This framework substantially handicapped the movement against Muawiya, because the goal of the Progeny (a) was to defend Islam and battle against corruption – not engage in what would be observed as a family fued.

Lack of Good People

It is not peculiar that those who joined the Commander of the Faithful (a) in battle had members that were loyal and members that were not. Those who were loyal were characteristic of sacrifice and putting their lives on the line. Thus, many of them were martyred in those battles. The others, however, were more reserved and less willing to sacrifice. Having no loyalty, they sold their allegiance to Muawiya as soon as the price was right. With many of the loyalists killed in battle and so many individuals with no loyalty and no principle, Imam Hassan (a) did not have much to rely on. Islam was in danger considering the lacking in this regard. The Progeny (a) were particularly cognizant of this fact and felt it a priority to preserve the blood of the little loyalists that remained in order to safeguard the faith.

IMAM HASSAN'S OPTIONS

It has become clear that the Imam (a) was living in very difficult circumstances, and thus the options he had before him were few. In fact, he only had two options.

Continuing on the Path of Battle Until Death

Imam Hassan (a) was far from inexperienced in battle. He knew war and he knew battle. He was at the forefront of every battle defending the honor of Islam and the Commander of the Faithful (a). The problem was not a question of whether or not Imam Hassan (a) was able to engage and lead militarily – he was more than capable by his mere experience, wit, and leadership qualities – it was rather a question of whether or not he could accomplish his principled goals, be it by military victory or martyrdom.

It is clear that it was not in the best interests of the Imam (a) to engage further in battle, due to the complexities and challenges we discussed earlier. If he were to engage in battle against Muawiya it would not have been any more effective than Ibn Zubayr's campaign against the Umayyads, which was a series of battles designed to gain power and reach the helm.[10] Taking this route, Imam Hassan (a) would

---

[10] Ibn Zubayr led a movement against the Umayyads in an effort to unseat the Umayyad caliph of the time – Marwan ibn Al-Hakam. His revolt, and the battles

have been simply seen as another character hungry for power who was killed because of his ambitions. Thus, even his martyrdom would not have been effective to instill change or reform and achieve the goals of the Progeny (a). He would not have had the desired impact on society given that Muawiya was able to buyout even the closest person to Imam Hassan (a) – Ubaydallah ibn Al-Abbas. This was in addition to many of the tribal chiefs who sold their loyalty and showed Muawiya that they were ready to hand over Imam Hassan (a) at any moment's notice.

Thus, the option of battle was a losing option no matter what. The only victory that could be realized was a military one. But such a victory would mean nothing since Imam Hassan (a) would not be able to realize his principled goals. Muawiya would have managed to employ his propaganda machines to turn any result of the battle into his favor through media campaigns and winning people over through payouts. The Imam (a) pointed to this reality when he said,

> By God, I did not agree to this truce except for the lack of supporters. For if I had supporters I would have fought him day and night, until God would judge between him and I. [11]

Peace Accord with Muawiya

The second option was striking a truce with Muawiya and return matters to order so that corruption and deviance can be addressed. This was the right choice for the Imam (a)

---

that ensued, were for the mere desire to gain power and dominion under the guise of vague claims of legitimacy.

[11] Al-Tabrasi, *Al-Ihtijaj*, 2:71.

whereby he was able to achieve a number of his goals, which can be summarized in the following:

One, Imam Hassan (a) prevented Muawiya from the opportunity to be seen as the peaceful loving leader to the people. Muawiya thought that surely if he were to present the truce to the Imam (a) he definitely reject it. Upon his rejection, Muawiya would come out to be as the one vying for peace while Hassan (a) would be seen by the people as a warmonger. So when Imam Hassan (a) did exactly the opposite and accepted the truce, Muawiya was caught off guard, forced to move forward with an accord and was unable to have his plan realized.

Two, through the accord Imam Hassan (a) was able to impose regulations on Muawiya – even though Muawiya did not abide by them completely – that would protect the interest of the believers. Muawiya was to stay clear of the followers of Ali (a) and that their lives, families, and property will be honored and unharmed. Though Muawiya did not honor this aspect of the accord and went on to have Imam Hassan (a) poisoned and killed a number of his companions, he was nonetheless limited by some extent by the accord. Given that there were now laws and regulations in place that protected the rights of the *Shia*, Muawiya was not able to sentence followers of Ali (a) to death as easily given that the discourse became more under the public's eye.

Three, through the accord the Imam was able to expose who Muawiya truly was to the people. He was exposed as a person that did not honor or respect agreements and accords given that he did not commit to the terms of the truce. It was clear that he had no interest in safeguarding faith or respecting its principles. On the first day he set foot in Kufa he announced to its people,

> *By God, I did not fight you so that you may pray or fast, so that you may perform pilgrimage or pay alms. I fought you because I wish to rule over you. God has given me that despite your wishes. I made a truce with Hassan and made him promises – all of that is under my feet for I will not honor anything of it.[12]*

Four, by Imam Hassan's (a) remarkable stance of wisdom, forebearance, and insightfulness he was able to set the foundations for the movement of Imam Hussain (a) and his martyrdom that revived the nation and safeguarded Islam. If it were not for the stance of Imam Hassan (a), which exposed the true face of the Umayyads, the rise and movement of Imam Hussain (a) would not have been successful. These two great Imams (a), Hassan and Hussain, fulfilled everything that they committed to in the peace accord with Muawiya, while Muawiya did not fulfill any element of his obligations in the accord. By the terms of the accord, Muawiya was obligated to hand over the caliphate back to Imam Hassan (a) but if Imam Hassan predeceased Muawiya then he would be obligated to hand it over to Imam Hussain (a). Thus, when Muawiya appointed his son Yazid he effectively have Imam Hussain (a) the perfect pretext and complete right to rise in his blessed movement. This is how Imam Hassan (a) was the driving force behind setting the grounds to show all the legitimacy, justice, and rightness of Imam Hussain's (a) movement – the movement

---

[12] Al-Mufeed, Al-Irshad, 2:14

of the Progeny, the movement against corruption, injustice
and tyranny.

BIOGRAPHICAL INFORMATION

Name: Hassan

Title: Al-Mujtaba

Kunya (Agnomen): Abu Muhammad

Father: Imam Ali

Mother: Lady Fatima

Born: Tuesday, 15th of Ramadan 3 AH (625 AD)

Birthplace: Medina

Died: Thursday, 28th of Safar 50 AH (670 AD)

Place of Death: Medina

Age at Death: 46

Gravesite: Jannatul-Baqi', Medina, Saudi Arabia

IMAM HUSSAIN
Eternal Renaissance

In the Name of God, the most Beneficent, the most Merciful

O you who have faith! Take recourse in patience and prayer; indeed God is with the patient. Do not call those who were slain in God's way 'dead.' No, they are living, but you are not aware. We will surely test you with a measure of fear and hunger and a loss of wealth, lives, and fruits; and give good news to the patient —those who, when an affliction visits them, say, 'Indeed we belong to God and to Him do we indeed return.' It is they who receive the blessings of their Lord and [His] mercy, and it is they who are the [rightly] guided.[1]

Imam Hussain (a) – the Master of Martyrs and the Leader of the Virtuous – a man that gave everything for God. He sacrificed every ounce of his being for the sake of God, no matter how small or how large, it was all for God. What Hussain (a) gave was what kept Islam and its principles alive. After the Umayyads tried everything to keep the

---

[1] The Holy Quran. Chapter 2 [The Cow; Arabic: *Al-Baqara*]. Verse 153-57.

words of truth silent, they were unable. *"They desire to put out the light of God with their mouths, but God will perfect His light though the faithless should be averse."*[2] The blood of Hussain (a) and his loyal companions was that essential agent that kept the light of faith brilliant from generation to generation.

We stand before the movement of Imam Hussain (a) and the massacre that took place in Karbala, bewildered by the gruesomeness experienced by the most pure of people. It takes us back to the the first crime witnessed by humanity – when Cain killed his brother Abel in cold blood – as the Holy Quran describes it:

> *Relate to them truly the account of Adam's two sons. When the two of them offered an offering, it was accepted from one of them and not accepted from the other. [One of them] said, 'Surely I will kill you.' [The other one] said, 'God accepts only from the Godwary. Even if you extend your hand toward me to kill me, I will not extend my hand toward you to kill you. Indeed, I fear God, the Lord of all the worlds. I desire that you earn [the burden of] my sin and your sin, to become one of the inmates of the Fire, and such is the requital of the wrongdoers.'*[3]
>
> *That is why We decreed for the Children of Israel that whoever kills a soul, without [its being guilty of] manslaughter or corruption on the earth, is as though he had killed all mankind, and whoever saves a life is as though he had saved all mankind. Our apostles certainly*

---

[2] The Holy Quran. Chapter 61 [The Ranks; Arabic: Al-Saff]. Verse 8.

[3] The Holy Quran. Chapter 5 [The Spread; Arabic: *Al-Maeda*]. Verse 27-29.

brought them manifest signs, yet even after that, many of them commit excesses on the earth.[4]

From the first crime of humanity to the numerous events of prophets of God being killed and oppressed as illustrated in the Holy Quran; still, no tragedy could compare to that of Karbala on the Day of Ashura. The worst of the crimes that took place, even against the prophets, people at the most interact with and are affected by them abstractly. With the tragedy of Hussain (a), however, God has given him a special place in the hearts of the believers. The heart does not tire from his remembrance no matter how frequent. Rather, the lamentation only increases whenever we remember him and attend the gatherings of his commemoration. People are able to restrain themselves and keep it together at the memorials of their loved ones, but with the memorials of Imam Hussain (a) and his family they cannot help but wail and lament. What is the secret about Hussain (a)? What are the reasons for Hussain's (a) tragedy being one that continues to live on from decade to decade standing the test of time?

It is essential to realize that the subject of Imam Hussain (a) cannot be understood if separated from the world of the unseen. The divine hand in this matter is clear. For the Holy Prophet (s) cried over him at his birth knowing of the tragedy that would befall him. The Commander of the Faithful (a) sorrowfully tells the tale of what will happen to his son Hussain (a) and his companions as he travels through the land of Karbala. In fact, some of our narrations tell us that all of our prophets have had some form of

---

[4] The Holy Quran. Chapter 5 [The Spread; Arabic: *Al-Maeda*]. Verse 32.

interaction with Karbala and knowing of the tragedy that Imam Hussain (a) would experience and the sacrifice he would make for Islam. If all of God's vicegerents knew of this tragedy, even before it took place, it is not strange that the memory would live on for thousands of years in the hearts of the believers and the faithful.

Nonetheless, there are a numerous elements beyond this that can possibly explain why Imam Hussain's (a) movement was so special and continued to live on – especially with the followers of the Progeny (a). These include: the humanitarian and ethical dimensions of the movement, the uniqueness in the brutality of the massacre, and the role of Imam Hussain (a) and his family in standing up against corruption.

HUMANITARIAN AND ETHICAL DIMENSIONS

This dimension was a working essential element in Imam Hussain's (a) movement because the primary goal of the movement was to shock and reawaken the moral conscience of the community. Probably one of the root causes of the absence or death of one's conscience is a defect in the ethics of the community. A community that is built on ethics and lives in accordance with ethics is a community that is alive in its conscience, and thus cannot be defeated. A community that has left its ethics, however, is a dead community no matter how large it becomes and how great its resources.

This ethical dimension is in fact one of the most important elements of all prophetic missions. The Holy Prophet (s) considered teaching ethics as a focal point of his mission, *"Indeed, I have been sent to perfect the best of ethics."*[5]

The most effective way to conquer and control a community is by killing its moral conscience. And that does not happen except by ridding the community of its principles, values and ethics. For a community that lives by the principles of honesty, loyalty, sacrifice, courage and generosity is one that cannot be dominated, controlled or conquered. You cannot play or toy with such a community. But when such a community loses these principles and values, its moral conscience dies along with any motivation to live a noble life. And in that case, such a community will accept anything in order to ensure its interests, desires and wants.

The focus of the Umayyads was to destroy the morals and ethics of the Islamic community. This is evidenced by Yazid's first speech upon becoming Caliph after his father Muawiya, luring people in through time off, money, relaxation and luxury:

> *...Muawiya used to take you on expeditions through the seas... and I will not be taking you on such expeditions... and keep you in the lands of the Romans during the winter, and I will not keep any of you in such lands in such harsh times... and he would give you your payments in thirds, but I will give that to you in whole lump sums.*[6]

---

[5] Al-Majlisi, Bihar Al-Anwar, 16:210.

[6] Al-Hakeem, Thawrat Al-Hussain (a), 141. Citing: Ibn Katheer, Al-Bidaya wal-Nihaya, 8:153.

And even clearer than this example are the words of Ibn Ziyad, Yazid's governor in Kufa, as he packaged the arguments to people to go out and fight Imam Hussain (a):

You found the Umayyads as your hearts please. And this is Yazid, you know him as one with a good, solid, praiseworthy path... he honors people and makes them rich with wealth... he increased your sustenance hundreds-fold... he is now ordering me to give you all these riches and take you out to wage war on his enemy Hussain... so listen to him and obey this command.[7]

Imam Hussain (a) would describe this painful reality that turned the Muslims from people who sought God and fought for His cause to people who are bought and sold with money. This was due to the fact that they lost their moral conscience, their will and and sold their afterlife for their limited pleasures in this world. The Imam (a) would tell his companions:

People are slaves to this world and religion is only words on their tongues. They hold on to it so long as their means of living are secured. But if they are tested with tribulation the true believers will be less... You see what has come upon us. This world has changed and become corrupted. What was commonly known as right has withered away. Nothing is left but a trace like the last few droplets of an empty cup and a lowly life like a tainted unwholesome pasture. Do you not see that truth [and righteousness] are not being acted upon [and abided by]? And that falsehood is not being discouraged? So let the believer long for meeting God. For I

---

[7] Al-Hakeem, Thawrat Al-Hussain (a), 141. Citing: Al-Muqarram, Maqtal Al-Hussain (a), 198-199.

114

do not see death [for God's sake] except as happiness, and
life with these oppressors except as weariness.[8]

From the aforementioned passages, the Imam (a) places his thumb on the wound. The corruption of ethics and the lack of moral values are the reasons that many Muslims stopped caring about religion and focused their attention only on matters of this world.

The Holy Quran and the noble narrations point to the importance of the ethical dimension of the life of the community, its advancement, and its happiness. The verses and narrations discuss the extent of harm that is brought to mankind by losing ethics. It moves people away from the grounds of nobility that God established for us. Furthermore, that loss changes individuals from servants of God to servants of this finite world, which will experience an end to its pleasures through its mere death.

In the movement of Imam Hussain (a), and his blessed renaissance, there was a focus on establishing a number of ethical principles. The goal was to broadcast these principles through the movement of Imam Hussain (a) and the effect it would have on the people in all of its dimensions. Similarly, these ethical principles were established in such a manner that they can be pointed to by humanity, across all the generations, and benefit from the light that is the movement of Hussain (a).

It is not possible to confine all of the ethical principles that Imam Hussain (a) practiced and established through his

---

[8] Al-Muqarram, Maqtal Al-Hussain (a), Pg. 192-193. Citing: Al-Tabari, Tareekh Al-Tabari, 4:305; Al-Andalusi, Al-'Uqd Al-Fareed, 2:312; and Al-Asbahani, Hulliyat Al-Awliya', 2:39.

blessed renaissance. However, we can point to some of the most important principles that no community should neglect. By holding on to the following principles and values, our communities can advance, move forward, and work along the godly path that God wished for humanity.

Honesty and Transparency

Honesty in our dealing with one another is among the most significant ethical principles that Imam Hussain (a) established. From the beginning of his movement, the Imam (a) did not give people false hope in spoils of war, well-being, or victory. Instead, he went against the norm of most political leaders who only cared for rallying the masses without regard to the reality facing the people, their conscience, and their intentions. Imam Hussain (a) was clear from the very beginning in the first announcement of his movement before leaving Mecca:

> *Praise be to God, everything is by His will, there is no strength save in God, and praise be upon His Messenger. Death is to the son of Adam like a necklace is to the neck of a young lady. O' how I long for my forefathers, like the longing of Jacob to Joseph. And I will meet the best of ends. Whoever would sacrifice his heart for us and is determined to meet God, let him journey with us for I am departing tomorrow morning God willing.*[9]

Imam Hussain (a) did not trick anyone or force anyone to go on his journey with him. He did not use the methods of the Umayyads in forcing people to fight or buying people's loyalty to militarize them and have them become soldiers.

---

[9] Ibid. 166.

Honesty and transparency are the features that distinguished Imam Hussain (a) and his companions from the rest of people. Initially, there was a huge group of people that followed Imam Hussain (a) thinking that he was going to take over the governance, as much of the matters were established for him completely. But then came the news of Muslim Ibn Aqeel, the ambassador of Imam Hussain (a) to Kufa. The people of Kufa had betrayed him, had him executed and ultimately broke their promise to support the movement of the Imam (a). Imam Hussain (a) did not keep this news from the people; rather, he shared it with them. He gave them the choice to stay or leave. Those initial large numbers dwindled down to a small group of loyal companions.

Imam Hussain (a) could have launched an all out marketing campaign to gain recruits by promising them riches and wealth. But that was not his character – he was honest with his men. As the heir of the Holy Prophet (s), there was no doubt he would establish these ethical principles and deal with reality instead of fraud and deception. This was the difference between The Progeny (a) and the military that stood against them. Probably one of the hardest stands that Imam Hussain (a) had to make was on the night of the tenth of Muharram. He gathered his companions and family members and said:

> I do not know of any companions better than my companions, nor a family more pure and rooted than my own. May God reward you on my behalf. I see that the day they will transgress against us is tomorrow. I give you leave to take off in the night, there is no blame or fault on you if

you leave. The night has shrouded you, so ride into the night. Let each one of you take a member of my household [as a guardian] and disperse in the lands and cities. May God reward you all. These people ask for me, not for you... and if they get to me they will be too preoccupied to go after anyone else.[10]

So the Imam (a) gave his companions and family members permission to leave him and did not force them to stay with him; rather, he relieved them of their duties towards him. But even with that, we find that this small honorable group refused to leave the Imam (a) and was determined to live and die beside him. Through this honorable stand, Imam Hussain (a) proved to us the necessity of leaders to live with their populace in a state of honesty and transparency. The leaders must not take advantage of their followers and supporters without their knowledge of the reality. Likewise, leaders must not take their followers for granted. This is extremely important in the validity of the movement and its advancement.

Sacrifice

Islam has given great focus to sacrifice and considers it among the noblest of ethical principles. It is enough that we see the Holy Quran point to this ethical virtue when God commends the Ansar for their stance with the Muhajireen and the sacrifices they made. God said:

[They are as well] for those who were settled in the land and [abided] in faith before them, who love those who migrate toward them, and do not find in their breasts any privation

---

[10] Ibid. 513.

*for that which is given to them, but prefer [the Immigrants]
to themselves, though poverty be their own lot. And those
who are saved from their own greed—it is they who are the
felicitous.*[11]

The history of Islam is filled, from its very beginning, with
wondrous stories that show that this particularity was
present in the midst of the Muslims. Many of them
espoused this honorable moral trait. However, the
weakening of ethical principles came as a result of
abandoning the teachings of Prophet Muhammad (s) and
turning away from the righteous guardians of the faith –
The Progeny (a). The many conquests that were undertaken
and the indulging in wealth and worldly pleasures could not
cover up the moral decay that had set in. Ethics were
further weakened by the Umayyads' role in dissolving and
ultimately eliminating the Muslims' adherence and
identification with moral virtues. This specific trait was
weakened just like other ethical virtues were weakened.

The school of Ashura came to reestablish this virtue,
whereby The Progeny (a) struggled in this pursuit with
Imam Hussain (a) and his companions at the forefront of
this struggle. They sacrificed themselves for the sake of
raising the word of God. As one poet says in Arabic,
"Giving oneself [as a sacrifice] is the epitome of generosity."
This is in addition to some of the phenomena that human
beings cannot fully comprehend and that can only be
produced by that holy household. That household was the
one that sacrificed for three consecutive days, as it fed the
poor, the orphan, and the prisoner and remained hungry.

---

[11] The Holy Quran. Chapter 59 [The Reckoning; Arabic: *Al-Hashr*]. Verse 9.

This is the household that birthed the likes of Al-Abbas (a), this hero who sacrificed for his brother and master Imam Hussain (a). He would head to the banks of the Euphrates river only to fill a satchel of water to quench the thirst of the women and children who had been without water for three days. Finally arriving, he kneeled down to take a sip of water. With all of his thirst and dehydration, he remembered the thirst of Imam Hussain (a) and the rest of the family. As he let the water go, it is reported that he said to himself:

O self, compared to Hussain you are nothing... and after him may you not live another day... this is Hussain coming close to his death... and you wish to drink the cold pure water? By God this is not an act of my faith.

Abbas did not drink in consolation of his brother Al-Hussain (a) and his family. Who could compare to the sacrifice and consolation of Al-Abbas (a) whereby he would prevent himself from drinking because his brother did not drink? He put his brother before himself and proceeded to return to the camp to get him water. Unfortunately he did not reach Hussain (a) or his family because he was killed by the treachery of Yazid's soldiers. This is one of many illustrations of sacrifice in the movement of Imam Hussain (a) and his companions.

Chivalry

Of the most noble and honorable virtues of Imam Hussain (a) was chivalry. He illustrated the highest forms of chivalry in his blessed revolution, which can be summarized in the following:

Imam Hussain (a) gave water to his enemies and their horses. The battalion of Al-Hur Al-Riyahi was ordered to stop the Imam (a) in Karbala before reaching Kufa. This battalion, loyal to Yazid, reached Imam Hussain (a) in such a dire state of thirst and dehydration. And they had come to stop the Imam (a). Nonetheless, when Imam Hussain (a) witnessed the thirst of his enemies, he ordered his companies to give water to the soldiers along with their horses. Who could compare to this show of chivalry? A man sees his enemies in such a weak state, knowing their plans against him, and with that he chooses to quench their thirst.

Al-Hur Al-Riyahi was responsible for much of the suffering that Imam Hussain (a), his companions, and family initially endured in Karbala. Regardless, the Imam (a) welcomed Al-Hur's repentance to God when he came forward on the Day of Ashura asking for forgiveness. On that day, Al-Hur looked at the two camps and saw Heaven and Hell. Pacing back and forth, pale in the face, he made up his mind and made his way to the camp of Imam Hussain (a) – he chose Heaven. Coming down from his horse, with his head bowed in shame, he called out: "O' God to you I turn, so accept my repentance. I have frightened the hearts of your loved ones and the children of your Prophet. O' Aba Abdillah, I am repenting... is there repentance for me?" Imam Hussain (a) replied, "*Yes. God will accept your repentance.*"[12]

This was the heart of Hussain (a). This was the heart so dear to the Messenger of God (s). A heart full of mercy, even to those who stopped him in Karbala. How could Hussain (a)

---

[12] Al-Muqarram, *Maqtal Al-Hussain (a)*, 182.

be any other way, when God made him the spiritual heir to the one sent as a Mercy to all Mankind?

Imam Hussain (a) was adamant on not starting the battle. He did not permit any of his companions to launch any arrows or spears at the enemy until the enemy launched first. Omar ibn Saad released the first arrow saying, "Witness for me before the Prince (Yazid) that I was the first to cast his arrow!" At that point, Imam Hussain (a) permitted his companions to respond. This was a true stance of chivalry and honor. Imam Hussain (a) could have easily taken preemptive measures and killed a number of Omar ibn Saad's soldiers; however, he refused to do anything of the like. His objective was to establish value and virtue and he made a point not to be the one who started the fight. Value and virtue were victorious on that day.

The Imam (a) continues to establish and consolidate these moral values like loyalty, sacrifice, bravery, and nobility, amongst others. He is able to do so due to the eternal nature of his movement and renaissance. As long as he is remembered, these virtues and values will also be remembered. The memory of Hussain (a) will remain as long as this world exists. This is one thing that makes the words of Imam Hussain (a) so true: *"Whoever does not follow me will not realize victory..."* What victory is greater than being eternal in memory and principle? Thus, these ethical virtues and godly principles will remain forever in his remembrance. Let every human being live in the love of Hussain (a) as he longs to follow his example of values and ethics.

THE BRUTALITY OF THE MASSACRE

As we stand before the details of the tragic memory of
Ashura, we find ourselves before a battle that has escaped
the measures of any other battle. One of the distinct
characteristics of this battle was the brutality that was used
against Imam Hussain (a), his companions, and his holy
family. History does not speak of a greater tragedy, nor do
we hear of any actions that have shamed humanity like the
crimes that were carried out against the family of the Holy
Prophet (s) and their companions. There are numerous
illustrations of these crimes written by historians. It is
possible to point in a general sense to some of the
illustrations of the horrid crimes executed by the enemies of
God against His Messenger and humanity. They became a
notorious gang that are damned by God, his angels, history,
and everyone who has an atom's worth of humanity in their
hearts. They disgraced humanity through their crimes that
will forever be etched in history. Of the many disgraceful
crimes that took place, we will illustrate a few through this
brief summary.

Imam Hussain (a), his companions, and family members
were all banned from drinking water. The women and
children suffered from dehydration for over three days.
They had committed no crime for which to be punished.
This painful image is crowned with Imam Hussain (a) going
out into the battlefield with his newborn child. He holds his
child up high for the entire camp of the enemy to see. He
tells them, "*If the adults have a sin [to answer for], then what is the
sin of the children?*" They refused to give him water. So, he
told them to take the newborn baby and give him water

themselves. To that request, the army fell into a dispute. Some of the soldiers expressed some compassion and said that they should give the baby ater. The others, however, remained cold and screamed out rejecting the request of the Imam (a). Omar ibn Saad ordered Harmala ibn Kahil Al-Asady, "End the dispute of our soldiers." As one of the best archers in the army's ranks, Harmala understood the message. He took an arrow and aimed it, not at Hussain (a) but at the newborn child. With that arrow he slaughtered the youngest son of the Imam (a). As the child's blood flowed from his neck, Imam Hussain (a) caught the rivers of red in the palm of his hand and cast the blood into the sky. *"Not one drop ever fell,"* said Imam Al-Baqir (a).[13]

What pains the heart even further is the illustration of how Imam Hussain (a) himself was killed. It is difficult to put pen to paper and remember the atrocity in its detail. They were not satisfied with just killing him. Rather, they rode their horses over his body ensuring that the hooves of their Arabian steeds pounded his blessed chest. They severed his head from his body and placed his head on a spear.

They burned the tents of Imam Hussain's (a) family, knowing that all the men had been killed, except for the ailing son of Imam Hussain (a). All that remained were women and children. They terrified the children and had them running between the flames that lit the tents in that callous desert.

Every scene is more tragic and heart-wrenching than the next. The more we see the more we are shown the reality

---

13 Ibid, 272.

that these people's hearts were dead and their conscience lost.

Even some of the enemies themselves could not hold their tears back when witnessing some of these scenes. The enemies' ferociousness did not differentiate between young or old. Anas Al-Kahili (ra) was an elderly man who came to support Imam Hussain (a) in his movement. Because of his frail body he used to wrap his turban around his waist to help straighten his back in an effort to stand firm against the enemies. When Imam Hussain (a) looked at him, the Imam (a) cried. Anas was not spared. Mercy was not shown to young men, a nursing baby, veiled women, or little girls either. What kind of human beings were on the other side of the battlefield and what kind of hearts did they have? They are a manifestation of the verse, *"Then your hearts hardened..."*[14]

Soldiers who stood on the other side of the battlefield themselves described the heinous crimes committed – Hameed bin Muslim, for example. As the Arabic saying goes, "With your own words, I condemn you." Another significant portion of the narrations come from the Progeny (a) whose truthfulness is undoubted by any Muslim.

Were those who committed such heinous crimes inflicted with spiritual and psychological diseases bringing them to carry out their crimes? Throughout history, in the present and the future, we will find these examples of people whose consciences are dead and hearts emptied of mercy and

---

[14] The Holy Quran. Chapter 2 [The Cow; Arabic: *Al-Baqara*]. Verse 74.

turned to stone. What are the reasons that caused these people to lose their humanity?

The Holy Quran points to this reality of dead and hardened hearts through a number of frank and direct verses.

Damnation is not limited to those who participated in the massacre of Imam Hussain (a) and his companions. Our pure Imams (a) supplicate to God in condemning and damning those who participated, those who were pleased, and those who followed the path of the killers of Imam Hussain (a). Take this passage from Ziyarat Warith for example, "*So, may God curse the people who killed you. And God curse the people who persecuted you. And God curse the people who were pleased when they had heard of that.*"[15] Also in Ziyarat Ashura:

> *May God condemn and damn the people who killed you. May God condemn and damn the abettors who instigated and had a part in your murder. I turn to you and God, away from them, their henchmen, their followers and their friends. O' Aba Abdillah, I pray and invoke God to send blessings upon you. I am at peace with those who make their peace with you; I am at war with those who go to war against you, till the Day of Judgment... I ask God, who honored you above others, to be generous towards me on account of you, and give me the opportunity to be with the victorious Imam (a) from the Household of Muhammad (s)...*[16]

---

[15] Al-Shaheed Al-Awwal, *Al-Mazar*, 124.
[16] Ibid. 179.

THE ROLE OF THE PROGENY

One of the most significant agents in the spread of Imam Hussain's (a) cause in the popular conscience of the people was the role played by the Imam's (a) family. They were able to bring his cause out as the truth that it was – a cause for Islam and reviving the tradition and principles of the Holy Prophet (s).

The immaculate members of the Progeny (a) did not live and die for the cause of Imam Hussain (a) because of an emotional familial attachment. They didn't spread this message so people could feel sorrow for them and extend their sense of empathy; on the contra, people's connection to their tragedy came because it emanated truth, sacrifice, chivalry, principle, and honor. The Progeny (a) sacrificed everything they had for this cause and made sure that the whole nation knew of it because it was part and parcel to the survival of Islam.

The renaissance of Imam Hussain (a) was central to protecting the religion of Islam and reviving the principles it was founded on. The divine messages sent to us from above have always faced movements that wished to be rid of the religion of God. When these movements were unable to annihilate the faith, they tried to steer people away from it. This is clear from the numerous divine religions that passed and the travesties they faced. God says,

> The Jews say, 'Ezra is the son of God,' and the Christians say, 'Christ is the son of God.' That is an opinion that they mouth, imitating the opinions of the faithless of former times. May God assail them, where do they stray?! They

have taken their scribes and their monks as lords besides God, and also Christ, Mary's son; though they were commanded to worship only the One God, there is no god except Him; He is far too immaculate to have any partners that they ascribe [to Him]![17]

Imam Hussain (a), and after him his sister Lady Zaynab (a) and son Imam Zayn Al-Abideen (a), stood against the movement that wished to destroy faith and attachment to God.

LADY ZAYNAB AND THE RENAISSANCE

When we think and reflect over Imam Hussain (a) there is an essential issue that is so inherent to this discussion – the stance of Lady Zaynab (a). She was Imam Hussain's (a) counterpart in his revolution. She was one of the intrinsic secrets to this grand mission that made Hussain's (a) revolution eternal in the hearts of every generation that followed. Zaynab (a) became like her mother Fatima (a) – a role model for all women in illustrating the essential role of women in bearing responsibility and sacrifice for the Word of God. We note that even though Lady Fatima's (a) modesty prohibited her from ever even entering the gatherings of men, when the greater good of Islam dictated that she stand boldly to call out the oppression done to her husband she did so courageously. She endured all that she endured, until she passed as an oppressed martyr who died for truth and principle. Lady Zaynab (a), the daughter of Fatima (a), took on a similar burden, responsibility and

---

[17] The Holy Quran. Chapter 9 [The Repentance; Arabic: *Al-Tawba*]. Verse 30 – 31.

sacrifice. She left her home and traveled from country to country, taken as a captive of war, all for the sake of a principle she believed in. That principle, that cause, was more beloved to her than anything in this world.

Zaynab (a) played a monumental role in her brother's revolution. She was the mouthpiece to the events that took place, the blood that was shed, and the sacrifices that were made. She told the world the story of Ashura – the day that Hussain (a) and his 72 companions gave their lives for the principles of their faith. Without Zaynab (a) we would not know about the greatest sacrifice and the most profound oppression experienced by the Holy Prophet's (a) household.

It is important to realize that Zaynab's (a) role cannot be summarized by the generic role played by women mourning the men they sent off into battle. Though Zaynab (a) undertook the responsibility of caring for the families that Hussain (a) and his martyrs left behind, her role was greater than that of a mere caretaker. Her role was no less than those warriors that fell as martyrs along with her brother Hussain (a), if not greater. In her position she was able to realize the goals of the revolution and achieve the objectives her brother set out to accomplish. Her role can be understood through the following points:

ZAYNAB: ROLE-MODEL FOR THE AWARE

Adamant Supporter

Zaynab went with Imam Husain (a) knowingly and willingly. She had all the proper excuses to remain in Medina, having a family, a home, a husband, and children. Nonetheless, she took permission from her husband to go with Imam Hussain (a) and went on that journey.

Someone could say that maybe Zaynab (a) did not know about her fate and what would transpire from her brother's revolution. And if she did know she would not have embarked on that journey.

History tells us that Ibn Abbas came to Imam Husain (a) and urged him not to leave Medina for his journey to Iraq. Imam Husain responded that this is the will of God and reform must take place. Ibn Abbas told him then don't take your family and women with you. To that Imam Husain (a) replied by saying that his grandfather, the Messenger of God (s), ordered him to take them with him and that he would never go against an order by God's Messenger (s). During the conversation, Ibn Abbas heard crying behind him in the other room. The crying turn into a voice that said,

> Ibn Abbas, you want our Master and Imam to leave us here and go on alone by himself? No, I swear by God, that we live only with him and we will die with him, for has time left anyone for us but him?

Upon hearing those words Ibn Abbas could not hold his tears and began sobbing.[18] That voice was the voice of Zaynab (a).

This short story tells us clearly that Zaynab (a) was fully aware of what this journey with Hussain (a) entailed. She made her decision to support and join her brother with this

---

[18] Al-Naqdi, *Zaynab Al-Kubra*, 140

awareness and eagerness to sacrifice for the principles of God. Zaynab (a) became the exemplar of a purposeful, mature, aware woman that moves throughout life with a mission and goal in mind. She did not embark on the journey with her brother out of necessity or out of a feeling of social responsibility that she was burdened with. She knew what role she was going to play and accepted the greatness that she would embody. She would come to be the one to stand before the tyrants and speak the words of truth and justice. She would let the words of truth ring wherever she would go. It was Zaynab that silenced the oppressors as she spoke and had the masses waiting on her next word, as if she were the Commander of the Faithful (a) in the flesh.

History also tells us that it was as if Zaynab's role in the revolution of Imam Hussain (a) was foreseen and planned for. Some historians note that when Imam Ali (a) married his daughter to her husband Abdallah ibn Ja'far he ensured that a condition in the marriage contracted included that Abdallah would never prohibit Zaynab (a) from travelling with her brother Hussain (a) when she chose to. This points to the divine will that designed for Zaynab's (a) role in the revolution – a revolution that rejuvenated the spirit of Islam and restored its teachings and principles.

Zaynab (a) and Sacrifice

Zaynab (a) was not satisfied with her role in the revolution of Hussain (a) without offering as many sacrifices as she could. She gave her son Aoun as a martyr for the principles that Hussain (a) rose for. Sacrificing your son is surely not an easy task. A mother could possibly endure every hardship except seeing her son slaughtered and beheaded before her very eyes. But Zaynab endured. With her deep conviction and faith she gave everything she had for the sake of God.

Let us not forget the contributions and sacrifice of Zaynab's (a) husband Abdallah Ibn Ja'far (may God be pleased with him) in his solidarity and support of Imam Hussain (a). Abdallah orderd his sons to join Imam Hussain (a) in his journey to be at his side in representation of their father. When Abdallah was later informed that his sons, Muhammad and Aoun, were killed he was sitting in his home. People began coming over to pay their respects and mourn the young men. Abdallah's servant, Abu Lislas, said, "This is what we received from Hussain." Abdallah scolded Abu Lislas and said, "You wretched man! To Hussain you say this?! By God, if I were with him I would not leave him until I was killed in his hands. My sons were good men. It is easier on my heart knowing that they were killed at the service of my brother and cousin – Hussain." Abdallah then turned to those present who had come to pay respects and said, "Praise be to God who honored me with the saga of Hussain. I was not able to support him with my own hands but I supported him with my own flesh and blood, my children."

Every household Zaynab (a) lived in – as a daughter in her parent's home and as a wife in her husband's home – was a house of sacrifice. These are the homes of the family of Abu Talib – Imam Ali's father – who stood for Islam and its Prophet from the very beginning. Thus, it goes without surprise that Lady Zaynab (a) and her husband would so willingly give their children to defend the principles of faith and protect the religion of Muhammad (s). The family of Abu Talib made a covenant with God to water the tree of Islam with their own sacred blood.

ZAYNAB (A) AND HER ROLE

Zaynab's participation in the revolution of Imam Hussain (a) can be divided into two primary points:

Involvement Prior to the Battle. Lady Zaynab (a) was fully involved in the battle that came with Imam Hussain's (a) revolution. She was briefed on all the developments that took place and was sought for consultation on strategy, tactics, and the course of action moving forward. Imam Hussain (a) did not keep her in the dark on any single issue. She had her role, her opinion and her say. Lady Zaynab (a) was in the events as they unfolded; thus, she was able to tell of all the details that took place from the battle of Karbala, especially from within the camp of Imam Hussain (a). The Imam (a) would give Lady Zaynab (a) his will and bid her the responsibility of being the caretaker for the all the orphans of Karbala. Most importantly he would assign her the responsibility of taking the verdicts and decrees of Imam Ali Zayn Al-Abideen (a), his son, and delivering them to the Shia – protecting him from the risk of persecution and oppression – according to some of our scholars.[19]

Her Role After the Battle. If we were to examine Lady Zaynab's (a) demeanor and conduct before the end of the battle of Karbala we would see her in a characteristic state of deep sorrow and sadness. For the mere sight of her

---

[19] Review Al-Muqarram, *Maqtal Al-Hussain*, 218

brother Hussain (a) being killed it was a state of immense show of grief and emotion. Lady Zaynab (a) embraced the bodies of her fallen family members – her brothers, her sons, her nephews – and wept and wailed over their tragedy. However, after the battle ended Lady Zaynab (a) was seen as a monument of patience – unbreakable like a rock. She would place her hands below the body of the most beloved of God's creation to her – Imam Hussain (a) – and look to the heavens and say, "God accept this sacrifice from us."

Was it that Zaynab (a) was not patient during the tragedies of the battle and that God bestowed upon her patience as soon as Imam Hussain (a) was finally killed? The answer is as follows:

When Zaynab (a) was weeping and grieving over the fallen warriors of her family during the battle she was reacting in a perfectly natural way. Emotion and affection are manifestations of God's mercy. The Prophet (s) cried over his children, Ali (a) cried over Lady Fatima's (a) tragedy, and Imam Hussain (a) and Lady Zaynab (a) cried over their brother Imam Hassan (a). However, when it came to Imam Hussain's (a) tragedy Zaynab's (a) role shifted. When Imam Hussain (a) was killed the responsibility of leadership and strength became hers. Note that the expressions of grief and emotions from the Progeny (a) are directly connected to God. Their tears for the tragedies are only shed because it is what God approves of, and so long as Zaynab's (a) patience was for the pleasure of God she would be patient. Lady Zaynab (a) embodied this connection and adherence to God in all of her actions. Thus, we see the shift to patience due to her acknowledgement and acceptance of her needed role after her brother to continue what he set out to do. That mountain of patience that was Zaynab (a) continues to bewilder the world to this day. Her role can be understood in three dimensions:

Guardian to the Family. She had put protecting the family, the women and the children as a priority above all. After the massacre they witnessed and the psychological and physical abuse they endured, they needed someone to be strong for the fragile state they were in. Zaynab (a) was that strength. She would give individual attention to each child and every woman, especially the night after Ashura.

Protecting the Imam. Lady Zaynab (a) had to protect the life of Imam Ali ibn Hussain (a). She risked her life in numerous situations to make sure that the son of Hussain (a) – the continuation of the line of the Prophet's (s) progeny – would remain alive. When Shimr saw that there was still a son of Hussain (a) alive, after beheading the Imam (a), he went for the blood of Ali ibn Hussain (a). Zaynab (a) stood before him and said, "You won't get to him unless you kill me first." Her bravery was then again displayed in the court of Ibn Ziyad when the governor ordered for Ali ibn Hussain (a) to be taken and killed. She leaped and grabbed onto her nephew and did not let anyone near him. She knew who Ali ibn Hussain (a) was, she knew his role as the proof of God on Earth – the next Imam for the people and protector of God's message. She wasn't defending Ali ibn Hussain (a) for the mere fact that he was her nephew. Zaynab (a) risked her life time and time again because she was serving her Imam, the inheritor of the Prophet's (a) leadership and knowledge.

Spreading the Message. This was by far one of the most important roles that Lady Zaynab (a) played. Beyond letting the people know who she was in her own right, she had the role of telling the masses about the revolution and sacrifice of Imam Hussain (a). The Umayyads tried to paint the battle of Karbala as being a legitimate use of force by the government to crush a rebellion by Kharajites who had defied the religion and defied the state. Thus, many of the cities that Lady Zaynab (a), the women and the children were taken through, as captives of war, did not know who they were. Here came the role of Lady Zaynab (a). Wherever she went she would announce who she was and what family she belonged to. She would tell the people what happened to the grandsons of the Holy Prophet (s) and expose the Umayyads for the criminals and killers they truly were. By her brave speeches and outspoken advocacy she was able to ensure the failure of the Umayyads' plans to justify their oppression. That is why Yazid actually tried to make himself out to be innocent from the massacre of Karbala blaming it on Ubaydallah ibn Ziyad, his governor in Kufa. We are certain that if it were not for Lady Zaynab (a) and the women with her, the revolution of Imam Hussain (a) would not have been able to miraculously awaken the dead conscience of the nation and bring it back to life. The blood that was shed would have been lost without the nation knowing what tragedy took place, how Hussain (a) and his companions were massacred so gruesomely, and the crimes that the Umayyads carried out against the Progeny of Revelation (a).

From this brief overview we can see more clearly the monumental role of Lady Zaynab (a) and the sacrifices she made. By this very right we speak of, the Holy Prophet (s) said, "*Whoever cries over the tragedy of this girl, will be like the one who cries over her brothers Al-Hassan and Al-Hussain.*"

"Cries" here means to interact and be affected by her cause, not simply displaying emotion. Such an interaction would move us to take her as role model and example that we can live by.

BIOGRAPHICAL INFORMATION

Name: Hussain

Title: Al-Shaheed

Kunya (Agnomen): Aba Abdillah

Father: Imam Ali

Mother: Lady Fatima

Born: Thursday, 3rd of Sha'ban 4 AH (626 AD)

Birthplace: Medina

Died: 10th of Muharram 61 AH (680 AD)

Place of Death: Karbala

Age at Death: 57

Gravesite: The Shrine of Imam Hussain, Karbala, Iraq

IMAM ZAYN AL-ABIDEEN
Safeguarding the Nation's Spirit

In the Name of God, the most Beneficent, the most Merciful

When Al-Zehri, a narrator of prophetic traditions, would refer to Ali ibn Hussain (a) in a tradition he would say, "Ali Zayn Al-Abideen told me..." His companion Sufyan ibn Ayeena would ask, "Why do you call him Zayn Al-Abideen (the best of worshipers)?" Al-Zehri replied, "Because I heard Saeed ibn Al-Maseeb narrate that Ibn Abbas heard the Holy Prophet (s) say, '*On the Day of Judgment a caller will call out – where is Zayn Al-Abideen? On that Day, I will see my son Ali ibn Al-Hussain ibn Ali ibn Abi Talib (a) emerge from the ranks.*'"[1]

BACKGROUND

It isn't strange that this Imam (a) would be entitled, 'the best of worshipers', given all the hardship he endured and the forbearance he emanated. He witnessed the massacre of his father, his uncle, his brothers and friends before his

---

[1] Al-Sadouq, *'Ilal Al-Shara'i*, 1:230

eyes. He saw the horses trample upon their blessed bodies after they gave their lives in sacrifice for their faith. He saw the women and children of his family beaten, tortured, taken captive, dragged into the desert and tormented from city to city across Syria and Iraq. He too was tormented, tortured, and mistreated in the worst of ways. For the rest of his life the Imam (a) would always remember these painful experiences and would often be found in tears at their simple remembrance. Any time he sat to eat a meal or was offered a drink of water his tears would automatically roll down his cheeks. It is narrated that Imam Al-Sadiq (a) said,

> *Ali ibn Hussain (a) cried over Al-Hussain (a) for forty years. There wasn't a time that food was placed before him that he did not fall into tears. In one instance, a servant told him, 'May I be sacrificed for you O' son of the Messenger of God! I fear that you will perish [from all this crying]. The Imam (a) then recited the following verse:* 'I complain of my anguish and grief only to God. I know from God what you do not know.[2] *'I have never remembered the tragedy of the sons of Fatima (a) without being choked by tears.*[3]

The weight of all this pain and sorrow still did not prevent the Imam (a) from carrying out his duty and role as the leader of the Muslims and the protector of the Prophet's (s) message. The Umayyads had entrenched a status quo built by corrupt policies enfranchising bankrupt beliefs and a creed foreign to the Islam of Muhammad (s). Through a

---

[2] The Holy Quran. Chapter 12 [Joseph; Arabic: *Yusef*]. Verse 86.

[3] Al-Sadouq, *Al-Khisaal*, 273

number of creative means that intelligently navigated this system that stopped at nothing to tarnish Islam and its protectors, the Imam (a) was able to safeguard the faith, promote its principles, and guide people intellectually and spiritually.

The Umayyads tried to rid the nation of Islam or at least deviate the Muslims from their practice of faith by proposing strange concepts and ideas, particularly in the two holy cities of Mecca and Medina. It's enough to go back to a book like Kitab Al-Aghani by Abi Al-Faraj Al-Asfahani to realize how the status quo in these two cities encouraged and became infested with corruption, entertainment, heedlessness, and immorality. Mind you this was existent even during the time of *hajj*. Those in authority propagated policies that encouraged and accepted behavior and activities that were against the teachings of Islam and its Prophet (s). They normalized forbidden activities in public like singing, dancing, drinking, amongst other things. The Imam (a) had a significant role to play in combatting this corrupt machine that was eroding people's attachment to the tenants of the faith. Imam Zayn Al-Abideen (a) aimed to correct the intellectual and spiritual state of the nation. Even with all the pain and hardship he faced in the gruesome massacre of his father along with the aftermath that followed, he did not give up on this sacred aim to redevelop the intellectual and spiritual foundation of the nation.

THE UMAYYAD MACHINE

The Umayyad politic threatened the intellectual and spiritual status of the Muslims. The intellectual foundations of ideology, creed and theology were at stake and so were the spiritual elements of ethics, behavior, and social interaction. These two dimensions can be detailed by the points that follow.

The Intellectual Threat

The Umayyads devised policies that would corrupt Islam from the inside. They employed pseudo-narrators to fabricate narrations and misinterpret the true meanings of the verses of the Holy Quran. They infiltrated the tradition of the Holy Prophet (s) in the psyche of the community. They held sermons, published and engaged in the social discourse with these new fabricated ideas – misleading the people from the true principles of the faith and replacing them with moral decay. The Umayyads' investment in such a fabrication campaign was done for two primary objectives:

1. To stray people away from truth and take vengeance on the Holy Prophet (s). The Umayyads only had envy and animosity for the Holy Prophet (s). They were the 'freed slaves' after the conquest of Mecca, in which Abu Sufyan and the Umayyads only submitted to Islam because they wanted to survive. Abu Sufyan swore enmity towards the Prophet (s), which carried on through his son Muawiya and his son Yazid.

2. To legitimize their own behavior that was in contradiction to Islam. When the Umayyads were at

the seat of the caliphate they found themselves at odds with the immaculate tradition and character of the Prophet (s). If people were to see such a stark contrast they would definitely rise against the Umayyads. So, the Umayyads decided to change what was found in the tradition of the Prophet (s) so that in people's perceptions there would no longer be such a contradiction. When an Umayyad caliph was found in gatherings of music, dancing and entertainment it wasn't a shocker, because the Umayyads' hired narrators had fabricated stories that the Prophet (s) also enjoyed such gatherings. These pseudo-narrators fabricated so many disgusting narrations about our Holy Prophet (s), which still have an impact on people's impressions of Islam today.

The vast number of converts at the time created an unstable environment given the diverse backgrounds and cultures of those coming to Islam. Though diversity and culture is celebrated in Islam, it was fertile ground for the Umayyads to induce their own "culture" into the mix of the confusion without being detected as outside of the new cosmopolitan norm.[4] This threat should not be belittled because it directly hits the core of legislation in Islam and what is forbidden and permissible. Instead of holding on to what the Prophet (s) legislated by divine order, the Umayyads enfranchised this take-all approach that adopted ideas and customs on baseless grounds. This had a profound impact on Islamic thought. When we go back to disciplines of jurisprudence

---

[4] Al-Sadr, Introduction to *Al-Saheefa Al-Sajjadiya Al-Kamila*, 9.

and thought we see how the notion of verdicts by opinion was popularized and ushered in this era. The danger of this new culture should not be taken lightly as it has numerous negative ramifications that continue to affect society today.

The third threat was the danger of the new ideological and theological beliefs that the Umayyads brought forth, especially their notion of predestination. The Umayyads used the idea of predestination – that we have no free will and God is fully responsible for our actions and choice – to free themselves from liability and accountability before the people for the injustices and crimes they committed. This strange concept was notably preached by Muawiya and then used by Yazid ibn Muawiya in claiming innocence from the massacre of Karbala when civil unrest grew against him. Muawiya famously said, "By God I did not fight you so that you may pray or fast, so that you may perform pilgrimage or pay alms. I fought you because I wish to rule over you. God has given me that despite your wishes."[5]

Notice how Muawiya attributed his matter to God, in that it was God who put him in this place of tyranny to rule over his subjects. Take a look at another time where Muawiya diverts the oppression that he is responsible for to God instead: "God says, *'There is not a thing but that its sources are with Us, and We do not send it down except in a known measure.'*[6] Then what do you blame me for if I have not given you enough?"[7] Nevertheless, there will always be those who will

---

[5] Al-Isbahani, *Maqatil Al-Talibeen*, 45

[6] The Holy Quran. Chapter 15 [The Rocky Tract; Arabic: *Al-Hijr*]. Verse 21.

[7] Abdul Hameed, *Tareekh Al-Islam Al-Thaqafi wal-Siyasi*, 769. Citing: Al-Zemkheshry, *Rabee' Al-Abrar*, 683.

stand up against oppressors and reveal the falsehood in their words. Al-Ahnaf ibn Qays would cleverly reply to Muawiya in that gathering and say, "By God, we do not blame you for what is in God's sources but rather for what He sent to us from His sources. You took what was ours from God and placed in your possession. You stand between us and Him."[8]

They say that the apple does not fall far from the tree. Yazid followed the same suit as his father Muawiya. After the massacre of Ashura, Yazid explains the killing of Imam Hussain (a) to some in his gathering. "Do you know where the son of Fatima (a) came from and what was the reason for the misfortune that befell him?" Yazid asks his gathering. They simply responded, "No." Yazid explained,

> *He asserted that his father was better than my father and that his mother, the daughter of God's Messenger (s), was better than my mother. He claimed that his grandfather was better than my grandfather and that he was better than me and even more deserving than I of this [caliphate]... his claims come from the lack of his understanding. He did not read,* 'Say, 'O God, Master of all sovereignty! You give sovereignty to whomever You wish, and strip of sovereignty whomever You wish; You make mighty whomever You wish, and You degrade whomever You wish.[9] *And when God says,* 'and God gives His kingdom to whomever He wishes...[10] [11]

8 Ibid.

9 The Holy Quran. Chapter 3 [Family of Imran; Arabic: *Aal Imran*]. Verse 26.

10 The Holy Quran. Chapter 2 [The Cow; Arabic: *Al-Baqara*]. Verse 247.

This idea was pushed to the extent of advocating for the notion that God does not record any misdeeds or sins for the caliphs. A conversation that took place between Waleed ibn Abdul-Malik, the 6th Umayyad caliph, and Al-Zehri is narrated by Ibn Abedrabboh. He says,

> *Al-Waleed ibn Abdul-Malik said to Muhammad ibn Shehab Al-Zehri that the people of Sham narrate that God only writes the good deeds and does not write the sins of those who are in authority over his subjects. Al-Zehri responded, 'That is a false narration. Is a caliph who is a prophet nobler before God or a caliph that is not a prophet?' Al-Waleed agreed that a caliph who is a prophet is nobler. Al-Zehri continues by saying that God says to His prophet David (a),* 'O David! Indeed, We have made you a vicegerent on the earth. So judge between people with justice, and do not follow your desires, or they will lead you astray from the way of God. Indeed there is a severe punishment for those who stray from the way of God, because of their forgetting the Day of Reckoning.*[12] If this is God's promise to His caliph prophet, then what do you think would be for the case of a caliph who is not a prophet?*[13]

This line of thinking had a stronghold in Sham – Greater Syria – and continued to spread across the Muslim world. The state built this ideology and adopted it as part of its

---

[11] Ibn Katheer, *Al-Bidaya wal-Nihaya*, 8:212.

[12] The Holy Quran. Chapter 38 [Arabic: *Saad*]. Verse 26.

[13] Abdul Hameed, *Tareekh Al-Islam Al-Thaqafi wal-Siyasi*, 771. Citing: Ibn Abedrabboh, *Al-'Aqd Al-Fareed*, 1:46.

creed. Whoever opposed it would be punished – a number of scholars were executed for voicing their opposition against this newly enfranchised nonsensical belief. Take the example of Ghilan Al-Dimashqi who was executed under the order of the Hisham ibn Abdel-Malik, the 10th Umayyad caliph, for this very reason. This baseless idea that was adopted into the creed of the Umayyad state is perhaps one of the single most dangerous intrusions into the faith as it continues to be blindly adopted and practiced today.

The Spiritual Threat

This threat upon the spiritual status of the Muslim nation came with the expansion of the Islamic empire and the many conquests that took place during the Umayyad dynasty. During this time the empire became richer day-by-day and material gain was the focus of society. The priorities of the community changed and there was an overall emphasis on money, power, entertainment and leisure. Worldly pleasures became the standard and the much revered simplicity of the life of the Prophet (s) was a thing of the past. Sin became so common in the public sphere that shame and bashfulness was seen as strange. People did as they desired and had little remorse for their actions. It was about the 'now' and how to make sure that those pursuits for money, women, entertainment and luxury was satisfied. A society that once bravely held the banner of truth and the pursuit for God became a society that raced towards the carnal desires of this world and all the fake glitter and glamor that comes with it. Instead of competing for knowledge, intellectual success, and spiritual gain people were racing towards indecency and sin. Instead of attending the mosque and staying up for night prayers they spent their nights in lewd gatherings, dancing, drinking, and filthy entertainment. Mecca and Medina were no longer cities characterized by sanctity and worship – the people infested the two holy cities with the worst of activities, which were sponsored and encouraged by the Umayyad state.

This is what Imam Ali Zayn Al-Abideen (a) stood up against. Still, he did not let it stop him from his immaculate mission to protect the message of the Prophet (s) and revive the people's intellectual and spiritual death.

The Imam's (a) strategic approach to protect faith and face the dangers brought forth by the Umayyads can be split into two primary objectives:

1) *Spreading Islamic Knowledge*
2) *Building the Spirituality of the Muslims*

SPREADING ISLAMIC KNOWLEDGE

The Imam (a) started an intellectual movement that would come to oppose the false ideas that were popularized with the Umayyads, to bring society back to the sacred teachings and creed of Islam. Our scholars tell us of this movement and its approach with the people. The Imam (a) – in the words of our scholars –

> *started a study group for teaching and research in the mosque of the Holy Prophet (s), where he taught people a variety of Islamic sciences including Quranic exegesis, narration, jurisprudence, whereby he would overflow them with the knowledge of his pure fathers. He trained the attentive amongst this group to be jurists and graduated a*

148

significant number of scholars. It was from this study group that the schools of jurisprudence flourished as it was the foundation of his active movement...[14]

Imam Zayn Al-Abideen (a) was able to insert himself in the intellectual arena even though the political situation was not conducive to him at all. While the caliphs and governors of the time did not approve of Zayn Al-Abideen (a), it did not stop students and scholars from gathering around the Imam (a) to learn and benefit from him even if they did not follow him as an imam. It is enough to see that even the caliph Abdul-Malik ibn Marwan praised the Imam (a) in saying,

O' Aba Muhammad, knowledge is apparent from your aura. The good that comes from you by God is overflowing, as you are part and parcel of the Messenger of God (s) and so close in his lineage. You are of an honorable purpose and of noble favor to both your family and your era. You have come with virtue, knowledge, faith, and wisdom that no one has come with before except from your family...[15]

The scholars held Zayn Al-Abideen (a) in such high esteem that they would not leave from Medina to Mecca until he did, out of respect and praise of him. Saeed Ibn Al-Maseeb narrates, "The scholars did not leave towards Mecca until Ali ibn Hussain would. So when he went so did a thousand others..."[16] There are numerous books that spoke to Zayn Al-Abideen's (a) knowledge and wisdom in the context of the intellectual arena, like *Al-Ihtijaj* by Al-Tabrasi which

[14] Al-Sadr, Introduction to *Al-Saheefa Al-Sajjadiya Al-Kamila*, 10.
[15] Al-Majlisi, *Bihar Al-Anwar*, 46:56. Citing: Ibn Tawoos, *Fath Al-Abwab*, 170.
[16] Ibid, 83:226. Citing: Al-Kashi, *Rijal Al-Kashi*, 108.

discusses the stances of the Imam (a) against the false ideas that were popularized during his time.

BUILDING THE SPIRITUALITY OF THE MUSLIMS

Supplication was by far one of the most important methods that the Imam (a) used in rebuilding the spiritual connection of the Muslims after they had been numbed by so much material indulging. In writing and teachings supplications, in addition to his unique dedication to worship, the Imam (a) became known and addressed as Sayyid Al-Sajideen (the Master of Postrators) and Zayn Al-Abideen (the Best of Worshipers). Promoting the culture of supplication had a huge effect on the community. It was a peaceful way to oppose the socio-political corruption that was taking place as well as the new culture of disgraceful ideas that had become widespread. The supplications that the Imam (a) taught connected people on a whole new level, educated them, and refocused their priorities to what was delivered by the Holy Prophet (s) – ultimately bringing people closer to God. The following are a few significant points that show us that.

Supplication as a Tool to Derail False Ideas

The Imam (a) was able to stand against the concept of predestination that the Umayyads promoted through the supplications he taught. Through the words of the supplication the supplicator would fully admit and take responsibility for their own actions before God. He would acknowledge that he was the one who went towards the sin and chose it without being forced by anyone. This spiritual and intellectual awareness destroyed any kind of objective reliance on the concepts that the Umayyads supported which they tried to promote to legitimize their own tyranny, oppression, and injustice. The Imam (a) was able to address these issues both theoretically and practically through the culture and education of supplication. In Al-Saheefa Al-Sajjadiya – a compilation of the psalms of the Imam (a) – one of the supplications read,

> *And will my admittance to You of the horrid things that I have done save me... Rather I speak from the position of the disgraced servant who has oppressed himself and taken lightly the sanctity of his Lord...[17]*

In the famously known supplication, Dua Abu Hamza Athamali, the supplication reads the heart wrenching words:

> *I am the one who did not revere You I sinned in my seclusions, nor did I observed Your commands in public. I am the possessor of the great craftiness of bad intentions. I am the one who challenged his Master. I am the one who disobeyed the Commander of the skies. I am the one who awarded the briberies upon the disobeying of the Magnificent. I am the one who when I was forewarned of the sin, I hastily raced to it. I am the one whom You awaited but I did not comprehend. You veiled my secrets but still I was not bashful, and I continued to commit sins belligerently insisting on it... O' my Lord! I did not disobey You when I did because I reject Your divinity, or because I belittle Your commands, or that I was daringly challenging Your punishment, or that I did not appreciate Your*

---

[17] Al-Saheefa Al-Sajjadiya, Supplication #13, 66

forewarning... Yet the mistake has occurred, and my self misled me, and my sinful desires won over me, and my misery helped me to it... For I have disobeyed You and opposed You with my own will, and now from Your retribution who will rescue me...[18]

Focusing on Understanding the Correct Creed

The Imam (a) spent a great deal of focus on spreading the correct beliefs and creed of Islam – particularly on the principles of the oneness of God, divine justice, prophethood, imamate, and resurrection – through the supplications he taught. Take note that in every one of the Imam's (a) supplications, he focuses much on the usage of the short prayer *"Allahuma Salli 'Ala Muhammad wa Ale Muhammad"* – may God send His peace and blessings upon Muhammad and the family of Muhammad. This is in itself is a clear foundational theological tenant. It naturally connects the Muslim to the Prophet (s) and his family in the best state that person can possibly be in – the spiritual connection with God. This is in addition to raising the community in acknowledging the significance of that short prayer and the role it plays in having our prayers and supplications answered.

Addressing All the Ailments of the Soul

With all the supplications that Imam Zayn Al-Abideen (a) wrote and taught, it was as if he was creating a supplication for every state of spiritual illness experienced by a human being. That is exactly what he did. There are various types of spiritual diseases, and each of his supplications worked as

---

[18] Al-Tousi, *Misbah Al-Mutahajid*, 589.

a specific medicine for that different type of disease or illness. The supplications varied from repentance, asking for ease, and protection from harm to having patience through trials and giving us strength. Moreover, the path to spiritual growth towards God is also on different levels. Thus, you will find specific supplications or psalms by the Imam (a) for "the Ascetics", "the Repenting", "the Frightened", and others directly related to the state that a person is in.

Supplications in Finding Oneself

The Imam's (a) supplications played, and continue to play, a significant role in allowing people find themselves and realize their dependence and humility before God. Money and power can make us feel independent and in no need. These supplications ground us and bring us back to reality, realizing our complete need and dependence on God Almighty. There is nothing more beautiful than to sit before one's Lord with the genuine feeling of complete submission to the One you need and are completely dependent upon — for without Him nothing could be. In that realization, we find our true richness, wealth and power. In other words, the supplications take us out of the farce of material power and wealth that many of us live in to come to the true wealth and power that lies with God. Zayn Al-Abideen (a) breaks our ego and the falsely enriched sense of self and moves us away from committing some of the gravest sins against God and ultimately against ourselves.

Connecting the Nation Back to God

Imam Zayn Al-Abideen (a) was fundamental in connecting people back to God, reminding them of what is most important, and acknowledging and appreciating the infinite blessings and favors that we enjoy. While people are easy to fall heedless and forget the blessings of God by being busy with the world and its glamor, the Imam's (a) teachings through his supplications alone reawakened people to realize that it is all temporary and that God is everlasting. This was the goal that the Imam (a) ultimately set out to do – bring people back to God. With all the obstacles and hardship, that is what he did and that is what he continues to do every single day.

BIOGRAPHICAL INFORMATION

Name: Ali

Title: Zayn Al-Abideen

Kunya (Agnomen): Abu Muhammad

Father: Imam Hussain

Mother: Shahr Banu (daughter of Yazdeger III, the King of Persia)

Born: Saturday, 15th of Jumadil-Awwal 36 AH (658 AD)

Birthplace: Medina

Died: 25th of Muharram 95 AH (717 AD)

Place of Death: Medina

Age at Death: 58

Gravesite: Jannatul-Baqi', Medina, Saudi Arabia

IMAM AL-BAQIR
The Keeper of the Progeny's Knowledge

In the Name of God, the most Beneficent, the most Merciful

It is He who has sent down to you the Book. Parts of it are definitive verses, which are the mother of the Book, while others are metaphorical. As for those in whose hearts is deviance, they pursue what is metaphorical in it, courting temptation, and seeking its interpretation. But no one knows its interpretation except God and those firmly grounded in knowledge; they say, 'We believe in it; all of it is from our Lord.' And none takes admonition except those who possess intellect.[1]

All of our Immaculate Imams (a) are models of the highest forms of excellence and perfection. Yet each of them went through a set of circumstances and acted accordingly, whereby each was able to showcase his prophetic characteristics in a distinct manner.

Because of that, we can look at each one of our Immaculate Imams (a) and draw a distinct number of lessons and gain

---

[1] The Holy Quran. Chapter 3 [Family of Imran; Arabic: *Aal Imran*]. Verse 7.

insight through contemplating on their different experiences.

Imam Muhammad ibn Ali Al-Baqir (a), the fifth of our Immaculate Imams (a), was known for his knowledge and wisdom. His circumstances allowed him to showcase the knowledge that he inherited from the Prophet (s) and spread the teachings of Islam and the Ahlulbayt.

Yet by looking at the life of Imam Al-Baqir (a), we do not only learn about his knowledge as an individual. Rather, we learn about the knowledge that all of our Immaculate Imams (a) possess, as they inherit these prophetic qualities throughout the generations.

HIS NICKNAME

Our fifth Immaculate, Imam Muhammad ibn Ali ibn Al-Husayn (a), is popularly known as Al-Baqir (a), a nickname given to him because of his vast knowledge and wisdom. In Arabic, the verb *baqara* means to bring forth in large quantities or to dig deep in the earth. Our Imam was nicknamed Al-Baqir (a) because he dove deep in the knowledge of this world and the hereafter, and brought out to us many treasures which we could not have reached.

Of course, this nickname wasn't given to him by his followers or simply by men who enjoyed the wisdom that he offered them. Rather, it was a divine trust granted to him through the Prophet (s).

It is narrated that the Prophet (s) told his companion Jabir ibn Abdullah Al-Ansari, "Oh Jabir! You will live until you meet a descendant of mine through my son Husayn (a). His

name will be Muhammad (a) and he will bring forth
[knowledge of] the faith in mass. When you see him, pass to
him my peace and greetings."

In another narration, the Prophet (s) adds "He is known in
the Torah as Al-Baqir (a)."[2]

A DEBATE WITH HISHAM

Imam Al-Sadiq (a) narrates that in one of the years, while he
and his father (a) were in the Hajj, Imam Al-Baqir (a) stood
and said in a sermon,

> Praise be to God who sent Muhammad (s) as a Messenger
> of Truth! And who honored us with [His Messenger (s)!
> We are the Chosen Ones of God's creation and His select
> servants. We are His vicegerents on earth. Glad tidings to
> whoever follows us! Wretched is the one who opposes us!

When news reached Hisham ibn Abdulmalik, the Umayyad
caliph of the time, he became consumed with envy. He
quickly dispatched a letter to Imam Al-Baqir (a) asking him
to come to Damascus. Imam Al-Baqir (a) and Imam Al-
Sadiq (a) came to Damascus and – after three days of
waiting for an audience – were allowed summoned to the
court of Hisham.

Hisham had set his court up with targets and invited the
chieftains of the Umayyad clan to practice in his court.
When Hisham saw Imam Al-Baqir (a) approach, he
welcomed him and asked him to participate in the archery.
Hisham, knowing that Imam Al-Baqir (a) had reached an

[2] Al-Qummi, Muntaha Al-Aamaal, 2:114.

old age, thought that he could disgrace the Imam (a) by beating him in archery.

Imam Al-Baqir (a) tried to excuse himself from the situation, but Hisham declined. When the Imam (a) saw that there is no convincing Hisham to excuse him from the match, he took the Umayyad chieftains on their offer.

The Imam (a) took the bow and launched the first arrow, landing an exact bullseye. He launched a second arrow and struck the back of his first arrow, splitting it in half. One after the other, the Imam (a) launched nine arrows, each splitting its predecessor in two equal halves.

Hisham became consumed with rage. He tried to hide his envy and said, "You have done well and you are the best archer amongst Arabs and non-Arabs! How can u claim that you've grown too old for archery?"

Hisham then brought the Imam (a) to the fore of the courtyard and sat next to him. He said to the Imam (a), "Quraysh will continue to rule over the Arabs and non-Arabs so long as people like you are amongst us. By God, tell me, who taught you to aim like this and at what age?"

Imam Al-Baqir (a) allowed Hisham a chance to save face and said, "I saw that the people of Medina had taken up the sport, so I began to train in it at an early age."

But Hisham did not get the hint. He continued to push and said, "I have not seen archery like this since I was born! I did not even think that there is anyone on earth that could aim like this! Does your son Jaafar (a) know how to aim like you?"

Seeing that Hisham was not willing to turn back and was adamant on having this debate, Imam Al-Baqir (a) said proudly,

We inherit the excellence and perfection that God granted to his Prophet (s) when He said, 'Today I have perfected your religion for you, and I have completed My blessing upon you, and I have approved Islam as your religion.'[3] *The earth will never be empty of someone who will carry these perfections that the rest of you lack!*

Upon hearing this, Hisham became consumed by his anger. He said grudgingly, "Aren't we, the bloodline of Abdmanaf, of the same lineage?" Imam Al-Baqir (a) replied, "*Yes, it is so. But God, majestic in his praises, has chosen us for His hidden secrets and the distillation of His knowledge – things which He has not granted to anyone but us.*"

Hisham retorted,

Did God not send the [the Prophet] Muhammad (s) from the bloodline of Abdmanaf to all humanity – black, white and red. So how could you inherit this in lieu of the rest of humanity, when the Messenger of God (s) was sent to us all? And that is what God declared in His words, 'To God belongs the heritage of the heavens and the earth.'[4] *So how did u inherit this knowledge when there is no prophet after [the Prophet] Muhammad (s), and you cannot claim to be prophets?*

Imam Al-Baqir (a) replied,

---

[3] The Holy Quran. Chapter 5 [The Spread; Arabic: *Al-Maeda*]. Verse 3.
[4] The Holy Quran. Chapter 3 [Family of Imran; Arabic: *Aal Imran*]. Verse 180.

It is from the words of God to His Prophet (s), 'Do not move your tongue with it to hasten it.'[5] He did not move his tongue to speak it to anyone but us, when God commanded him to bestow it upon us and not on anyone else. That is why he took his brother Ali (a) as his confidant rather than any other companion.

God then revealed a verse of the Quran in that regard and said, 'and that receptive ears might remember it.'[6]

The Messenger of God (s) said, 'I asked God to make [that receptive ear] yours, oh Ali (a).' That is why Ali ibn Abi Talib (a) said, 'The Messenger of God (s) taught me a thousand chapters of knowledge, each chapter containing another thousand chapter.'

So just as God chose His Prophet (s), the Prophet (s) chose his brother Ali (a)to be the holder of the treasured secrets of knowledge that were not given to anyone else. This is how it came to us, and why we pass it through our generations [of Immaculate Imams] without sharing it with the rest of our family.

Hisham could not control his envy and anger. He burst, "Ali (a) claimed that he had knowledge of the unseen, while God did not share that knowledge with anyone. So how can he make such a claim?"

Imam Al-Baqir (a) replied calmly,

God, majestic are His mentions, revealed to His Prophet (s) a book that contained knowledge of all the events that have passed and all that will come to pass until the day of judgement. God described this when He said, 'We have

5 The Holy Quran. Chapter 75 [The Resurrection; Arabic: *Al-Qiyama*]. Verse 16.
6 The Holy Quran. Chapter 69 [Arabic: *Al-Haaqqa*]. Verse 12.

sent down the Book to you as a clarification of all things and as guidance, mercy and good news for the Muslims. [7] *In another verse, He says,* 'and We have figured everything in a manifest Imam' [8] *And in another verse, He says,* 'We have not omitted anything from the Book.' [9]

Then God revealed to His Prophet (s) not to leave anything of his knowledge of the unseen, hidden secrets, and treasured insight, except that he should pass it on to Ali (a).... The Prophet (s) then said to his companions, 'Ali (a) will fight for the interpretation of the Quran just as I have fought for its revelation.'

Indeed, no one possessed the entirety of the Quran's interpretation but Ali (a). That is why the Messenger of God (s) said, 'the best in judgment amongst you is Ali....'

When Hisham saw that he could not beat Imam Al-Baqir (a), asked him for whatever he wished. The Imam (a) said, "*I left my family and close ones and they are worried for my absence.*" So Hisham grudgingly granted his wish and allowed him to head home. [10]

This was not the only such debate that Imam Al-Baqir (a). He was known for his debates and dialogues with all kinds of individuals, including scholars from other faiths. Because of the short nature of this treatise, however, we will leave the details of these debates and suffice ourselves with what we have mentioned thus far.

[7] The Holy Quran. Chapter 16 [The Bees; Arabic: *Al-Nahl*]. Verse 89.
[8] The Holy Quran. Chapter 36 [Arabic: *Ya Seen*]. Verse 12.
[9] The Holy Quran. Chapter 6 [The Cattle; Arabic: *Al-An'am*]. Verse 38.
[10] Al-Qummi, *Muntaha Al-Aamaal*, 2:147-50.

KNOWLEDGE OF HIS FOLLOWERS

The knowledge that the Imam (a) was entrusted was far greater than what we could imagine. As he himself said in the story we mentioned earlier, "*knowledge of the unseen, hidden secrets, and treasured insight.*" But of that knowledge, perhaps what is most important to us is the knowledge of the Imam (a) of his followers.

Abu Basir narrates that, while sitting in a gathering with Imam Al-Baqir (a), an African man walked in. The Imam (a) asked, "*How is Rashid?*" The man replied, "I left him alive and well, and he sent his peace and salutations." The Imam (a) replied, "*My God have mercy on his soul.*" The man was dumbstruck. He asked, "Did he die?" The Imam (a) replied, "*Yes… Two days after you left him.*"

Abu Basir narrates that he asked Imam Al-Baqir (a) about the man. The Imam (a) said, "*He was one of our followers and a lover [of our bloodline].*" The Imam (a) then turned and said,

> *Do you think that we do not see you or hear you? Pity on such a [mistaken] opinion! By God, there is nothing hidden from us from your deeds. Remember us always. Train yourselves to do good deeds. Be amongst the good-doers and you will be known. This is my advice to my children and followers.*[11]

Of course, we do not mention these narration here to show that Imam Al-Baqir (a) was special – relative to the rest of the Immaculate Imams – in this knowledge. But as we said before, we study his immense knowledge to gain an

---

[11] Al-Qummi, *Muntaha Al-Aamaal*, 2:127.

understanding of the knowledge that all of our Imams (a) possess.

This knowledge that the Imam (a) has of his followers is applicable to all Imams (a). Knowing this, let us contemplate on the fact that our Twelfth Holy Imam (a) has this encompassing knowledge of all of our deeds. He knows where we go and what we do. He knows what we say and what we conceal in our hearts and minds.

He is closer to us than we could image.

Can we say that we please him with our actions? Can we say that we are proud of all that he knows of us?

If not, how can we reform ourselves to please him and be amongst his followers?

BIOGRAPHICAL INFORMATION

Name: Muhammad

Title: Al-Baqir

Kunya (Agnomen): Abu Ja'far

Father: Imam Ali Al-Sajjad

Mother: Fatima bint Al-Hassan

Born: Tuesday, 1st of Rajab 57 AH (677 AD)

Birthplace: Medina

Died: 7th of Dhil-Hijjah 114 AH (732 AD)

Place of Death: Medina

Age at Death: 57

Gravesite: Jannatul-Baqi', Medina, Saudi Arabia

IMAM AL-SADIQ
The Teacher of All Scholars

In the Name of God, the most Beneficent, the most Merciful

Before even delving into the life and character of this immaculate individual, it is such a blessed fact to observe that Imam Ja'far Al-Sadiq (a) was born on the very same day as his great grandfather – the Holy Prophet Muhammad (s). Perhaps it was divine will that wished for the remembrance of Imam Al-Sadiq (a) to be on the same day as the Holy Prophet (s), to give another show of the authentic proximity between these two individuals of excellence. Even further than that is the fact that Imam Al-Sadiq (a) held the titles that the Holy Prophet (s) was first known as amongst the people – Al-Sadiq (the Truthful) and Al-Ameen (the Trustworthy). Just like the Prophet (s), our Imam (a) was addressed by the people in the same way for his honesty and trustworthiness. In fact, the first to address him with such a title – before he was even born – was the Holy Prophet (s) himself. It is narrated that he said, *"And God will bring from his [i.e. Imam Muhammad Al-Baqir] progeny the word of truth and honesty."* To that the Prophet (s) was asked, "So

what is his name, oh Prophet of God (s)?" The Prophet (s)
replied, "*He will be called Ja'far, honest in his speech and conduct.
The one who hurts him is like the one who hurts me, and the one who
rejects him is like the one who rejects me.*"[1]

Imam Al-Sadiq (a) is a personality that does not divide the
Muslims; rather, his words and conducts brought them all
together. Thus, he should be celebrated by all of us –
regardless of sect or faction – because he called us to path
of the Prophet (s) and battled the deviant ideologies and
philosophies that aimed to bring divide in the nation of
Muhammad (s). Moreover, the blessed fact for the
proximity between this Imam (a) and the Holy Prophet (s)
naturally induces discussion to return to the remembrance
of our Holy Prophet (s). For whenever we mention or
remember Imam Al-Sadiq (a) we are bound to remember
and discuss the virtues, leadership and honor of the Holy
Prophet (s).

In this regard, out of the many virtues and attributes of
Imam Al-Sadiq (a) there are two fundamental virtues from
his life that make him unique and like his grandfather the
Prophet (s). This is not to say that the rest of the Imams of
the Progeny (a) – who are all one light, one guide, and one
school of thought – did not have this proximity to the Holy
Prophet (s), but rather that the circumstances of his time
allowed Imam Al-Sadiq (a) to stand out with these
characteristics.

These two fundamental virtues are knowledge and ethics.
Knowledge and ethics are the keys to realizing happiness

---

[1] Al-Khazzaz Al-Qummi, *Kifayat Al-Athar*, 83.

and the wings that allow the complete human being to ascend in his journey toward excellence. For knowledge without ethics is not enough for a person to realize excellence and the endless good for which he was created. Nor is ethics alone enough for us to ascend to the skies of goodness and happiness. Basically, you can't fly with one wing. Imam Ali (a) expressed, *"My back has been broken by two types of individuals: a licentious scholar and a monastic ignoramus."* A scholar who is without ethics cannot be a man of excellence; rather, he is a burden on Islam and the Imam (a) considers him to be of those who 'break his back.' At the same time, people who are ignorant yet hold on to ethics can't be attributed with excellence either. Thus, the Holy Prophet (s) and his grandson Imam Al-Sadiq (a) gave great priority and importance to these two foundations – knowledge and ethics.

ON KNOWLEDGE

The Holy Prophet (s) cared deeply for knowledge. In fact, the first word that was revealed to the Prophet (s) from his Lord was "Read." This word alone has so much significance, as the Prophet's mission was to bring people out of the darkness of ignorance into the light of knowledge and awareness. It is through knowledge that nations are finessed and human beings are distinguished from the rest of creation.

The Holy Prophet (s) emphasized the importance of knowledge so much that he even attached to it monetary value in addition to its given moral value. When a Muslim woman would marry and her husband did not have the means to give gift her with a dowry of monetary value, the Holy Prophet (s) advised to gift her the lessons of learning the chapters of the Holy Quran. Her dowry would be lessons in knowledge of the Quran – what more of a proof is it that knowledge reigns superior to any other gift.

The Prophet (s) emphasized knowledge so much that he wouldn't let any excuse stand in the way of seeking it. No matter how hard it is or how far you need to travel, you have to seek knowledge. We are mandated to educate ourselves, to learn, and seek knowledge. He said, *"Seek knowledge even if you have to go as far as China, for seeking knowledge is incumbent on every Muslim."*[2]

Imam Al-Sadiq (a) would go forward to dedicate his whole life to this noble purpose. Every hour and minute he had, he dedicated to help guide others from ignorance to knowledge. Some narrate that the scholars of the Mosque of Kufa amounted to be over four thousand, all of which would say, "I have learned from Ja'far ibn Muhammad that…" They would narrate from Ja'far ibn Muhammad in preference over other sources.[3] Muhaqiq Al-Hilli also states that, "From him – Imam Ja'far Al-Sadiq (a) – spread knowledge that fascinated the minds…"[4]

His knowledge and teaching was not limited to his followers; rather, it encompassed the entire Muslim community. The well-known founder of the Sunni *'Maliki'* school of thought, Imam Malik, described Imam Al-Sadiq (a), "No eye could see, no ear could hear, no heart could

2 Al-Nisabouri, *Rawdat Al-Waa'ithein*, 11.
3 Al-Ameen, *A'yan Al-Shia*, 1:35.
4 Al-Muhaqiq Al-Hilli, *Al-Mu'tabar*, 1:26.

witness a better human being than Ja'far ibn Muhammad in virtue, knowledge, worship, and wisdom. He was plenty in his wise discussion, gracious in his gathering, and abundant in the benefit he gave."[5] History does not mention any notable scholar at the time of Imam Al-Sadiq (a) who did not benefit and learn from the Imam (a). Take the following individuals as examples: Abu Hanifa, Ibn Abi Layla, Sufyan Al-Thawri, and others who are considered as scholars of jurisprudence and who studied under Imam Al-Sadiq (a).

Imam Al-Sadiq's (a) teaching was not limited to narration, jurisprudence, and the Quran. In addition to these fundamental sciences, he taught medicine, chemistry, mathematics, amongst other disciplines. Through his dedication the Imam (a) was able to bring back to life the teachings of the Holy Prophet (s) at a time that was infested with deviance and fraud. He brought the Muslims back to the correct authenticated narrations that clearly traced back through the immaculate Imams and finally to the Holy Prophet (s).

ON ETHICS

There is no doubt that ethics has a huge impact on the makeup and growth of every individual. Ethics are perhaps the single most important foundation upon which a person's character and personality are built upon. The ethics of the individual are what make up the ethics of a community, a society, and a nation. Thus, the Holy Prophet (s) gave this dimension of our lives so much importance. In

---

[5] Ibn Shahr Ashoob, *Manaqib Aal Abi Talib*, 3:372.

fact, he considered it to be the cornerstone of his message. *"I was sent to perfect the best of ethics,"* he famously said.[6]

Imam Al-Sadiq (a) carried on this torch of morality to guide people out of a dark period of ignorance that they had lived during the rise of the Umayyads after the Holy Prophet (s). Through his own example, he brought people closer once again to the same principles established by his grandfather Muhammad (s). He did not depend on the theories of philosophers and wise-men, he derived his inspiration directly from his immaculate fathers, the Holy Prophet (s) and the revelation of God – the Holy Quran. He was undoubted by all groups as the true exemplar of morals and ethics. As much as he was the teacher of knowledge and science, he was the father figure, the mentor, the guardian that raised the community by his own hand on the morals and virtues of his grandfather. Al-Sadiq (a) believed wholeheartedly that you could guide others without necessarily speaking. All you had to do was actually show the way. *"Call others toward you without your tongue."*[7] The best way to guide people is through action.

This advice proves to be even more instrumental to us in our day and age. When we are open to so many different cultures and societies and such societies are open to us. We need not to talk to each other about what we believe and where we come from. We need to show it through our conduct and behavior. If we truly believe that our faith is the path to guidance and salvation, we simply need to practice it. Like Imam Al-Sadiq (a) told us, we need to call

---

6 Al-Tabrasi, *Makarim Al-Akhlaq*, 8.
7 Al-Barqi, *Al-Mahasin*, 1:18.

onto others 'without our tongues.' This is not to say that we always remain silent; rather, it is to emphasize the importance of action over speech, fulfillment over empty promises, following through over incompleteness, integrity over hypocrisy. Imam Al-Sadiq (a) was not a man who simply spoke of theory; he was a practical, real-world, solutions-oriented leader. Perhaps one of the reasons that he continues to be remembered to this day is that there was no disconnect between the things he said and the things he did during his lifetime, as well as the effect such leadership had on society after him. There was complete harmony between speech and conduct, something characteristic God's vicegerents.

Their conduct is equal to their speech in regards to the legislative effect it has. This consistency that existed in God's representatives, was especially apparent in Imam Al-Sadiq (a). He did not behave morally simply in the public eye to gain favor and popularity amongst the people as a virtuous leader. He was virtuous all the time wherever he was, whether in the public eye or in the privacy of his own home.

BIOGRAPHICAL INFORMATION

Name: Ja'far

Title: Al-Sadiq

Kunya (Agnomen): Abu Abdillah

Father: Imam Muhammad Al-Baqir

Mother: Um Farwah

Born: Monday, 17th of Rabi'ul-Awwal 83 AH (699 AD)

Birthplace: Medina

Died: Monday, 25th of Shawwal 148 AH (765 AD)

Place of Death: Medina

Age at Death: 65

Gravesite: Jannatul-Baqi', Medina, Saudi Arabia

IMAM AL-KADHIM
Patience in the Tyrants' Dungeons

In the Name of God, the most Beneficent, the most Merciful

Indeed God chose Adam and Noah, and the progeny of Abraham and the progeny of Imran above all the nations; some of them are descendants of the others, and God is all-hearing, all-knowing.[1]

Imam Moussa Al-Kadhim (a) emerged after the decline of the Umayyads and the rise of the Abbasids. When the Abbasids ascended the caliphate, they came with the campaign of returning the right of power back to the grandsons of the Holy Prophet (s) – one that was unjustly taken by Muawiya and his fellow Umayyads. When power fell into their hands, however, they no longer advocated for the sons of Muhammad (s) and instead held onto the helm for hundreds of years thereafter. The peculiar thing is that the Abbasids – or Banu Abbas – were the cousins of the Imams (a). They are the descendants of Abbas, one of the Prophet's (s) youngest uncles.

---

[1] The Holy Quran. Chapter 3 [Family of Imran; Arabic: *Aal Imran*]. Verse 33-34.

Imam Al-Kadhim (a) went through a particularly challenging time with the rise of the Abbasids. What was seemingly a positive direction taken by Muslim community with the decline of the Umayyads, was instead a new era of oppression and injustice against the Progeny (a) of Muhammad (s). It was an age known to the Shia for its trials and tribulations, especially to the Imam of the time – Al-Kadhim (a). In fact, Imam Moussa (a) became known as 'Al-Khadim' – or the one who represses his rage – because of the severity of the oppression and terror he experienced and yet remained patient.[2]

In looking at the life of this great individual, we can examine and understand two essential issues that relate to the socio-political construct of the time:

1) The Reasons the Abbasids Turned on the Progeny (a)
2) The Mechanisms the Abbasids Used Against the Progeny (a)

ABBASID TREASON

Examining the biographies of all our Imams (a) generally, and specifically the biography of Imam Al-Kadhim (a), we see that the oppressors of their time always stood in opposition to them. This is even with the fact that the Imams (a) did not rise up in arms against the rulers of their time, nor did they call onto people to revolt and rebel against the caliphs. So why were the rulers opposed to the

---

[2] *Qabasat min Seeret Al-Qada Al-Hudat*, 2:94. Citing: *Mukhtassar Tareekh Al-Arab*, 209.

Progeny (a) and why did they fear this household to the extent that they felt the need to imprison, persecute, and even assassinate them?

For one, the rulers of the time knew who the members of this household were. They knew that the Imams (a) were the true heirs of the Holy Prophet (s) and were the sole individuals with right to the caliphate. So naturally, they lived in a state of anxiety with regards to the Progeny (a). So long as an imam from that family was alive, no matter how quiet or unthreatening the Imam (a) may seem, it would still bother the person at the helm and worry him. What is peculiar is that some Abbasid caliphs actually admired and respected the Imams (a) as the true leaders of faith, and yet oppressed them nonetheless.

Take the example of Al-Ma'moun ibn Al-Rashid. In one occasion, Al-Ma'moun would turn to some of his companions and say, "Do you know who taught me Shi'ism?" They would answer, "No, by God, we don't know." He replied, "Al-Rashid." Confused, his companions would ask, "How is that so when he ordered the killing of people from that household?" Al-Ma'moun replied,

> He killed them over power because power is vain. I went to hajj with him one year and when we arrived in Medina we entered in the dwelling we were going to be staying in. He ordered the guards saying, 'No man is allowed in whether he be from Mecca, Medina, from the Muhajireen or the Ansar, or from Banu Hashim or any of the tribes of Quraysh, except that he introduces himself and shows his lineage.' Upon that Al-Rashid would honor the guest with a generous gift. The time passed and Al-Fadl ibn Al-

Rabee' comes in saying, 'Master, there is a man at the door saying he is Moussa ibn Ja'far ibn Muhammad ibn Ali ibn Hussain ibn Ali ibn Abi Talib (a).' We were all present – Al-Ameen, Al-Mu'taman, myself and the rest of the commanders with Al-Rashid. When he came near we gazed upon him in awe of his prestige, his light, his immaculate aura. My father greeted him with open arms, embracing him and kissing his head and taking him by the hand to seat him next to him in the center of the gathering. He inquired about his state and seemed so genuinely engaged in discussing with Al-Kadhim (a). Finally when he excused himself from the gathering, my father got up with him and walked him out bidding him farewell. He came back and told us, 'Follow your uncle and master and assist him with whatever he needs.'[3]

In another narration, Al-Ma'moun was confused by the way his father acted towards Imam Al-Kadhim (a) and privately asked him why he honored and praised Al-Kadhim (a) in such a way. To that Al-Rashid would reply, "My son, he is the owner of the right [i.e. the caliphate or leadership]." Al-Ma'moun then asked, "If you know that then why don't you return this right back to him?" Al-Rashid would say, "It is power. By God, if you were to contest with me over it I would have your head..."[4]

Another reason the Abbasids took such a harsh stance against the Progeny (a) was that they were threatened by the natural popularity these Imams (a) gained with the people. Even those who did not profess to follow the Imams (a) –

---

[3] Al-Hassani, *Seerat Al-A'imma Al-Ithney Ashar*, 2:330.
[4] Ibid.

from laymen to scholars – would go back to them for advice, mentorship, and leadership. As the Imams (a) increased in popularity and likeability with the people for their knowledge, wisdom, charisma, and ascetic and humble lifestyle, the Abbasid leadership would be worried that the people would compare them to the Imams (a). A lavishly living, not so knowledgeable or religious caliph could not come close to this immaculate, wisdom-filled, charismatic imam. In addition to this, the Abbasids' campaign of claiming closeness to the Prophet (s) as descendants of his uncle was overshadowed by the Imams (a) closeness to the Prophet (s) as his grandsons.

It is narrated that Haroun Al-Rashid asked Imam Al-Kadhim (a), "Why have you made it permissible for the people to trace your lineage back as sons of the Holy Prophet (s)? You are the sons of Ali and a person should trace his lineage back to his father, and the Prophet (s) is your grandfather from your mother's side." The Imam (a) replied, *"I ask you, if the Holy Prophet (s) were to ask for the hand of your daughter would you accept?"* Al-Rashid answered, "Of course, and how could I not accept?!" Imam Al-Kadhim (a) then said, *"In my case, he would not ask for the hand of my daughter nor would I accept."* Puzzled, Al-Rashid asked why. *"Because I am his grandson and you are not."* Acknowledging the logic Al-Rashid exclaimed in commendation. Still, Al-Rashid asked,

But how could you say you are his progeny when a progeny is derived through a male and the Prophet (s) did not have any sons, and you are from the sons of his daughter? You must give me the proof for the sons of Ali, and you, O'

Moussa, are the imam of the time. I won't leave you until
you give me the proof from the Book of God.

Then Imam Al-Kadhim (a) recited the following verse,
"...and from his offspring, David and Solomon, Job, Joseph, Moses
and Aaron—thus do We reward the virtuous— and Zechariah,
John, Jesus and Ilyas—each of them among the righteous."[5] Here the
Imam (a) asked him, *"Who was the father of Jesus (a)?"* "He had
no father," Al-Rashid replied. The Imam (a) then said,

> *We trace the lineage of Jesus to the previous prophets (a)*
> *through his mother Mariam (a). In the same way, we trace*
> *our lineage to the Holy Prophet (s) through our mother*
> *Fatima (a)...*[6]

After the revolution of Imam Hussain (a), the Imams (a)
thereafter avoided political movements against the caliphs
of their time. They quietly and wisely dedicated to guiding
and teaching people, while protecting the principles of the
faith and standing up against ideological, philosophical, and
theological deviance. But even with their lack of patent
political opposition towards the caliphs, the Abbasids were
not satisfied. They wanted to be unopposed politically and
religiously. That is why you see across the history of the
Abbasids, and the Umayyads before them, such large
investments in religious scholars. So long as there was a
significant group of clerics on their side, legitimizing their
actions through skewed interpretations and amendments to
the faith, they were at ease. But the fact that the Imams (a)
did not rest when it came to creatively showing the people
truth from falsehood disrupted the Abbasids' strategy to

---

[5] The Holy Quran. Chapter 6 [The Cattle; Arabic: *Al-An'am*]. Verse 83-84.
[6] Al-Hassani, *Seerat Al-A'imma Al-Ithney Ashar*, 2:330.

maintain political and religious legitimacy. Take this short story as an example:

One day in Medina, Haroun Al-Rashid stood in front of the shrine of the Holy Prophet (s) and sent his salutations, "Peace be upon you O' Cousin!" His salutation was said in this way to show the people his closeness to the Prophet (s) and that he is more legitimate as an heir to the caliphate being a grandson of the Prophet's (s) uncle. The Imam (a) negated this fallacy in people's minds by showing his own closeness to the Messenger (s). He would step up to the shrine and say, "Peace be upon you O' Father!"[7] The Imam (a) constructively reduced any legitimacy the Abbasids claimed from this avenue. This of course aggravated the Abbasids and made them despise the Progeny (a) even more.

PLOTS AND MACHINATIONS

The Abbasids employed a number of mechanisms to belittle and hurt the Progeny (a) of the Prophet (s). One of the ways they tried to be rid of the Progeny (a) was by directly trying to kill them to cut off the lineage. The Abbasid caliph Al-Mansour wanted the heir of Imam Al-Sadiq (a) dead before he could claim imamate. So he ordered his representative in Medina – Muhammad ibn Sulayman – to keep his ear to the ground regarding the matter. Al-Mansour told him that if Al-Sadiq (a) chooses a successor to have the successor executed. Some days passed and Ibn Sulayman gives word to Al-Mansour that Imam Al-Sadiq (a) chose five successors: Al-Mansour himself, Muhammad ibn

---

[7] Al-Hassani, *Seerat Al-A'imma Al-Ithney Ashar*, 2:328.

Sulayman, his sons Abdallah and Moussa (a), and his wife Hameeda. When news reached Al-Mansour, he exclaimed, "If this is the case, then there is no way to eliminate his successor."[8]

Aware of the threat, Imam Al-Sadiq (a) averted their plan through this move. He knew that if they wished to kill one of these successors – or at least the Imam's (a) two sons – everyone would realize that the Abbasids were behind the murders. For one, the Abbasid dynasty had a reputation for slaughtering the descendants of Ali ibn Abi Talib (a). They were also the only party with a motive for these murders – they would be seen as trying to eliminate their rivals for the title of succession to the Imam (a).

Imam Al-Kadhim (a), saved by his father's wisdom, was nonetheless imprisoned more than eight different times by the Abbasids. The Abbasids did not oppose the Progeny (a) simply as a reactionary matter to the Progeny's (a) course of action in the social sphere. What crime did the Imams (a) commit against the Abbasid caliphs to instigate such oppression? No crime was committed nor did they threaten the caliphate from being unseated. Still, the Abbasids wished to be rid of the Imams (a) even before they officially assumed the position of imamate publically.

The Abbasid authorities chose to imprison Imam Al-Kadhim (a) to keep him away from the public light, removed from interaction with the people. They wanted to limit people's exposure to him and lessen the impression of his knowledge and leadership. But even in prison, the Imam

---

8 Al-Kulayni, *Al-Kafi*, 1:31.

(a) had a tremendous effect on those around him. His patience, forbearance, and contentment with whatever situation he was in was awe-inspiring.

Issa ibn Ja'far reports to Al-Rashid,

> *Moussa ibn Ja'far has prolonged in my prison. I have tested him and have kept him under watchful eyes. He does not leave the state of worship. I had my guards listen closely to what he says in his supplication. He did not mention you or me negatively in a single supplication. He only prays to his Lord for forgiveness and mercy. If it were up to me I would set him free as I am only ashamed.*[9]

The Imam (a) had so affected the guards and the ward of the prison that they were pleading for his release with the caliph.

Al-Rashid himself confessed that the Imam (a) was the pinnacle of faith and the exemplar of worship. When the Imam (a) was transported to another prison, within the vicinity of the Abbasid palace, Al-Rashid noticed something peculiar. Every day he would walk out on his terrace and see a pile of clothes lying on the ground below. He asked the groundskeeper, Al-Rabee' ibn Younis, why there was a pile of clothes lying there everyday unmoved. The groundskeeper of the prison said, "That is not a pile of clothes Master. That is Moussa ibn Ja'far. Everyday after sunrise he prostrates and remains in that state until sunset." Al-Rashid was baffled. "Indeed this is from the asceticism of *Banu Hashim*," he said in awe. Seeing that Al-Rashid was in awe of the Imam's (a) worship, Al-Rabee' told the caliph,

---

[9] Al-Mufeed, *Al-Irshad*, 2:240.

"O' Master, then why do you continue to torture him with imprisonment?" Al-Rashid replied simply, "Because it must be done."[10]

Another tactic used by the Abbasids was the attempt to overshadow the personality of Imam Al-Kadhim (a) by promoting other "scholars" in the limelight of the community. The Abbasids invested a great deal in a large group of scholars, paying them salaries to speak favorably of the state, and funding their research projects to presume legitimate functions before the people. These state-appointed scholars carried the agenda of the Abbasids and were used to divert people's attention from the true religious authority of the Imams (a). But how foolish could these rulers be that they think they could cast away the beaming light of the sun by raising their limp hands to the sky. God says, *"They desire to put out the light of God with their mouths, but God is intent on perfecting His light though the faithless should be averse."*[11] And in another verse, *"They desire to put out the light of God with their mouths, but God will perfect His light though the faithless should be averse."*[12]

This sacred light of the Progeny (a), Imam Moussa Al-Kadhim (a), was praised and admired by scholars who did not follow or believe in his imamate. The Hanbali Sheikh Abu Ali Al-Khelal said, "Whenever I had a need I would go to the grave of Moussa ibn Ja'far asking God by his right and God eased for me what I wished."[13] Ali ibn Muhammad

---

[10] *Qabasat min Seeret Al-Qudat Al-Hudat*, 2:104 citing to *Hayat Al-Imam Moussa ibn Ja'far*, 1:140-144, citing to Al-Majlisi, *Bihar Al-Anwar*, 48:220.

[11] The Holy Quran. Chapter 9 [The Repentance; Arabic: *Al-Tawba*]. Verse 32.

[12] The Holy Quran. Chapter 61 [The Ranks; Arabic: *Al-Saff*]. Verse 8.

[13] Al-Khateeb Al-Baghdadi, *Tareekh Baghdad*, 1:133.

ibn Ahmad Al-Maliki, also known as Ibn Al-Sabbagh, described the Imam (a) saying,

And of his nobility, favor, virtues and grace... it is only witnessed that he is the pinnacle of honor and highness. He ascended to the zenith of excellence and remained at its top. He rules over the spoils of glory, choosing the most pure of it and only purified it further...[14]

Kamal El-Deen Muhammad ibn Talha Al-Shafe'i said that Imam Al-Kadhim (a) was,

the great Imam with the magnificent will and undying resolve. He was the unsurpassed jurist known for his worship and virtue. He spent his nights in prayer and prostration and his days in fasting and giving charity. With all the pain he endured he was forbearing. He prayed for those who wronged him and asked God to forgive them. For how much he prayed he was called 'the Veracious Servant of God.' In Iraq, he is known as 'the Gate of Requests to God' for the rate of success of those who ask God by his right. His virtues boggle the mind and make it certain that he has with God an undeniable position of grace.[15]

Quotes like these praising the Imam (a) are many. How could you not praise something that is clear as day? Imam Al-Kadhim (a) continued to be sent from one prison to another until he was taken to the prison of Al-Sindi. There he was poisoned by the order of Haroun Al-Rashid. The Imam (a) was martyred, poisoned by the hand of his Abbasid cousins, remaining patient until his very last day.

---

[14] Ibn Al-Sabbagh, *Al-Fusool Al-Muhimma fe Ma'rifet Al-A'imma*, 937.
[15] Ibn Talha, *Matlab Al-Sa'ool fe Manaqib Aal Al-Rasool*, 477.

BIOGRAPHICAL INFORMATION

Name: Moussa

Title: Al-Kadhim

Kunya (Agnomen): Abu Ibrahim

Father: Imam Ja'far Al-Sadiq

Mother: Hamida al-Barbariyyah

Born: Sunday, 7th of Safar 128 AH (745 AD)

Birthplace: Abwa (between Mecca and Medina)

Died: 25th of Rajab 183 AH (799 AD)

Place of Death: Baghdad

Age at Death: 55

Gravesite: Kadhimiyan Shrine, Baghdad, Iraq

IMAM AL-RIDA
Content with God's Decrees

The 17th of the month of Safar marked the death of one of the greatest men that ever lived. One of the flagships of the Progeny, an honor to his forefathers, and a mercy to those in his midst – Imam Ali Al-Rida (a).

Like his fathers, he gave humanity everything he had of knowledge, wisdom, ethics, education, and guidance. His hands brought blessing to the period of history he lived in. His presence was undeniable and his leadership, despite all the challenges and hardship he faced, was mesmerizing.

When we look at the life of this Imam (a) we realize, like the rest of the Imams, two underlying characteristics from his life. One, constant oppression and animosity towards him and his family. Two, even with all the oppression and animosity, his enemies were unable to dissuade people from loving him and being in awe of his presence.

"Indeed We presented the Trust to the heavens and the earth and the mountains, but they refused to undertake it and were apprehensive of

it; but man undertook it. Indeed he is most unjust and ignorant."[1] What oppression is worse than for a person to oppress himself and inevitably create barriers between his person and his potential, his happiness, his success. For when we oppress others we are ultimately oppressing ourselves and throwing ourselves into an abyss of failure. Likewise, what ignorance is worse than the ignorance that pushes one to silence the truth and do away with knowledge. Such ignorance pushes one to envy. That envy drove Satan to disobey God and swear enmity against Adam and his progeny. That envy was the cause that drove Cain to kill Abel, his own flesh and blood. That envy brought so many woes to humanity and essentially ushered the oppression we mentioned above.

Nevertheless, as ignorance and envy coupled to produce oppression against the greats, it did not stop people from being evoked with love and affinity towards the greats of Muhammad's (a) Progeny. Though history was written by the hands of the enemies of the Progeny (a), and that public opinion was generally against them, we find that that same history is still full of virtuous mentioning of the Prophet's (s) family. There is no escaping it. Imam Al-Rida (a) and his likes were incontestable. That is why God says, *"They desire to put out the light of God with their mouths, but God will perfect His light though the faithless should be averse."*[2] No matter how hard the enemies of the Prophet (s) tried dissuade others from loving and admiring his progeny, people would only gravitate even stronger towards them.

---

[1] The Holy Quran. Chapter 33 [The Parties; Arabic: *Al-Ahzab*]. Verse 72.

[2] The Holy Quran. Chapter 61 [The Ranks; Arabic: *As-Saff*]. Verse 107.

Imam Al-Rida (a) particularly went through a great deal of oppression. Writing and reading about these incidents will allow us to further appreciate his leadership and give us lessons that we can live by. The purpose of remembering such oppression is not simply to feel emotional and cry over the tragedies the Imam (a) and the rest of his family went through. We remember so that we can strengthen our intellectual and spiritual foundation and fortify our souls against instigation, sedition, and deviance. We remember the principles that this Imam (a) lived and died for so that we may appreciate all that we have and guard ourselves from throwing it away through carelessness or thanklessness.

The individuals and groups that encountered the Imam (a) with oppression were diverse. It wasn't necessarily just one consistent group, there were many. Some were from aristocratic families that were known for their status, wealth and power. Others were close individuals to the Imam (a) that were originally pious, learned, and wise people. Unfortunately, their priorities changed and so did their character. Once knowledgeable, trustworthy, notable aides to the Imam (a) became oppressors to him. They sold their afterlife for this temporary life.

The Holy Quran's accounts of what happened to the communities of history is very consistent. History repeats itself. The difference is simply the time and the place. However, we see that people generally have the same tendencies, the same desires, the same ambitions and the same course of action. Still, we find it so shocking to hear the stories of our prophets and imams in how they were betrayed, oppressed, and even killed. We can't stomach the idea of how some of the Shia, the followers of the Progeny (a), dealt with the Imams of their time. How did they betray the Imam (a)? Why didn't they stand with him? Where were all the supporters? This questioning stands true from Imam Ali (a) and Imam Hassan (a) to Imam Hussain (a) in Karbala and the rest of the Imams. We need to ask ourselves, would we have behaved in the same manner the people of the time did? What would our position be? It is easy to speculate when we are safe from the test and trials, but if we were the heat of the action that took place how strong would our faith be? Would we doubt our Imam (a) when the whole world stood against him or would we stand firm unmoved in our conviction?

Learning about the experiences of the Imam (a) had and the oppression he faced will allows us to learn more about ourselves and how we would interact with the vicegerent of God. The trials he endured could be divided into three categories:

THE IMAM (A) AND HIS FAMILY

By far one of the most heart wrenching experiences is to have to endure oppression and injustice from the closest people to you. Imam Al-Rida (a) had this experience when some of his own siblings stood against him and accused him of terrible things. They accused the Imam (a) of keeping their late father's, Imam Moussa Al-Kadhim, money to himself and essentially stealing their inheritance. The fact that Imam Al-Kadhim (a) designated Imam Al-Rida (a) as his heir, successor, and the guardian over the affairs of the people after him, and did not designate his others sons made them envious of the Imam (a). It drove them to make unwarranted accusations against their brother and even bring the case before a judge. They argued that there was a chest that Imam Al-Kadhim (a) gave Imam Al-Rida (a). Within that chest was their father's will, some of his possessions, and jewelry and gems stashed at the very bottom that they argued they were entitled to. They complained to the judge that their brother Ali Al-Rida (a) wishes to take it all for himself and not share any of it with his siblings. Finally, the judge asked to have the chest opened and it showed that no treasure of jewelry and gems existed. All the accusations were false and fabricated. Nonetheless, Imam Al-Rida (a) still treated his siblings with respect and virtue.

The Imam (a) was the exemplar of ethics and virtue, that was his only option – to be a mercy to those around him – even if they were nothing but cruel to him. After the ordeal of accusations and the judge's ruling for the truth, Imam Al-Rida (a) did not stop at that. He turned to his siblings and said that even though he knew, as they knew, that their claims were baseless he was still intent on giving them what they wanted. He ordered one of his aides to gather a lump sum of money from the Imam's (a) own personal ownership and distribute it to his siblings. Even with such a noble and gratuitously generous gesture, they remained cruel and unpleasant towards the Imam (a). They continued to accuse him of groundless horrible things. His siblings went to the point of stirring doubt in his fatherhood of Imam Muhammad Al-Jawad (a). With all of that, the Imam (a) did not once reciprocate such terrible behavior. He only met them with kindness, graciousness and mercy. Whenever Imam Al-Rida (a) would travel outside of the city he advised his son Al-Jawad (a) to check on his aunts and uncles, to give provide them if they needed anything, and to never turn them away if they were to come to the Imam's (a) home. This was something that the Imams (a) continued to emphasize – maintaining strong ties with family – no matter what.

THE IMAM (A) AND HIS COMPANIONS

One of the most trying experiences Imam Al-Rida (a) faced was the split between his father's companions after his father's passing. Some of the closest companions to his father denied Imam Al-Rida's (a) imamate. Historians note that one of the primary incentives for this group of companions to reject Imam Al-Rida (a) was the fact that they were in control of sums of money and religious dues. Imam Al-Kadhim (a) was imprisoned by the Abbasid authorities for a long period of time. Thus, he arranged for his close companions to handle the religious dues and collect from the believers; this included *khums*, *zakat*, *sadaqa*, etc.

With the wealth that they had amassed from the believers, greed overtook these companions. They realized that if they recognized Imam Al-Rida (a) as the next Imam they would naturally be mandated to follow his instructions on how to handle that money. By rejecting the Imam (a) they gave themselves free reign to use it as they wished.

Thus, they announced that Imam Al-Kadhim (a) did not actually die, but had gone into *ghayba* (occultation) and was the Mahdi and the final Imam. They claimed that Al-Kadhim (a) will return one day as the awaited savior. Their greed had them fabricate this entire announcement which created a de facto off-shoot that became known as "*Al-Waqifa.*"[3]

Though they were few, some companions were not swayed by greed like the *Waqifa* companions. Take the example of Younis ibn Abdulrahman. Once he realized that Ali Al-Rida (a) was the rightful imam, he began advocating for his leadership and telling people to pay allegiance to Al-Rida (a) as the rightful successor of his father. A few of the *Waqifa*, like Ziyad Al-Qindi and Ali ibn Abi Hamza Al-Bata'i, tried to persuade Younis to stop advocating for Imam Al-Rida's (a) imamate. They promised him 10,000 *dinars* if he were to stop insisting on Al-Rida. Younis rejected their offer and refused to sell his religion like they had.

Money can take us to the worst of places, where we end up selling our friends, our family and our religion. Principles become secondary and we have no standard by which we make our decisions other than arbitrary pursuit for material gain. No matter how knowledgeable or pious we are, we should always be mindful of these temptations and guard ourselves with caution from falling into this horrid sin. We need to keep God as our priority and realize that anytime

---

[3] The term *Waqifa* is derived from the Arabic root *Waqafa*, meaning to stop. They were given this name because they stopped at Imam Al-Kadhim (a) and refused to accept the remainder of the Twelve Immaculate Imams (a).

we leave the path of light, the only alternative is the path of darkness and ignorance.

It is important to realize the way Imam Al-Rida (a) dealt with and addressed these companions that strayed and created their own group for their greedy pursuits. The Imam (a) damned them and described them as degenerate disbelievers and hypocrites. The reason for his approach here was that deviance from creed and religion knowingly was not a matter that the Imam (a) could be silent on.

It wasn't because they unjustly took huge sums of the Imam's (a) or the believers' money; recall the way the Imam (a) dealt with his family members who accused him taking their 'treasure'. Their accusations were baseless and still he gave them money. In this case, however, it wasn't an issue of money or personal insult to the Imam (a) that he could mercifully stand and forgive the *Waqifa*. Instead, it was an ideological and theological issue that these individuals were trying to deceive others into taking a path that they knew was wrong.

The Imam (a) had a responsibility to protect people and their faith from deviance; and thus, he ensured that such individuals were known for their true faces and would not be able to affect the vast majority of the believers. The Imam's (a) insistence on this shows us the deep importance of holding on to our creed and not being lenient in this regard. Our creed is our identity and our identity should never be tainted.

THE IMAM (A) AND THE ABBASIDS

Imam Al-Rida's (a) experience with the Abbasids was unique. Most of the Imams were tried with the rulers of the time in a relationship of outright oppression, persecution and subjugation. Imam Al-Rida (a), however, was tried in the caliph's attempt to make Al-Rida (a) a partner to his rule and successor to his throne. The caliph of the time was Al-Ma'moun Al-Abbassi. The caliph put the Imam (a) in a position whereby forcing him to accept the role of successor, with the hopes of accomplishing a few specific goals:

1) Tarnishing the reputation of Imam Al-Rida (a) and his place with the masses
2) Silencing the revolutionary elements within the followers of the Progeny (a)
3) Forcing the other Abbasids to fall in line by the threat of passing on the rule to a non-Abbasid

Imam Al-Rida (a) knew of Al-Ma'moun's intentions. Though Al-Ma'moun portrayed himself as wanting to give back to the Imam (a) what was rightfully his, the Imam (a) knew the greater scheme that was being played. Al-Rida (a) accepted to be the 'successor' with a number of conditions that were unexpected by Al-Ma'moun. The most important of these conditions was that the Imam (a) would refuse to be involved in any of the matters of governance. By making this condition, the Imam (a) was able to safeguard his leadership and reputation with the masses. The people would come to see the Imam (a) and instantly fall into tears for the status of their Imam (a) was clear – he was in a position against his wishes. There was no glamor or luxury that the Imam (a) sought. His choice to accept the position was only to safeguard the faith and the faithful.

Though Al-Ma'moun was able to silence much of the revolutionary elements by his move of assigning Imam Al-Rida (a) as successor, he was unable to tarnish the reputation of the Imam (a) with the people. The people realized what had taken place and that the leadership of the Imam (a) was not bound by an institution or government. It irked Al-Ma'moun that the Imam (a) was so admired by the people for his knowledge, virtue, and excellence. Realizing how more and more people were gravitating towards his new heir, the caliph became threatened for his own position of power. No matter what scheme that he could put in place he could not lower the stature of this man. Thus, Al-Ma'moun like the rulers before him decided to take the cowardice course of poisoning the Imam (a). Imam Ali Al-Rida (a) was martyred on the 17th of Safar in the year 203 AH.

BIOGRAPHICAL INFORMATION

Name: Ali

Title: Al-Rida

Kunya (Agnomen): Abul-Hassan

Father: Imam Moussa Al-Kadhim

Mother: Ummul-Banin Najmah

Born: Thursday, 11th of Dhul-Qi'dah 148 AH (765 AD)

Birthplace: Medina

Died: Tuesday, 17th of Safar 203 AH (819 AD)

Place of Death: Mashhad

Age at Death: 55

Gravesite: Shrine of Imam Al-Rida, Mashhad, Iran

IMAM AL-JAWAD
Ageless Leader

In the Name of God, the most Beneficent, the most Merciful

A flag from the unwavering flags of Islam, leader from the leaders of guidance, a monumental figure born out of the House of Revelation, a guiding light saving us from the darkness of our ignorance – he is the Ninth Imam of the Progeny of Muhammad – Imam Muhammad ibn Ali Al-Jawad (a).

Imam Al-Jawad (a) stands out from the rest of the Imams of the Progeny in that he took on the responsibility of *imamate* (leadership) at a very young age. Some historians say that he was 14 years old, while others contend that he was younger still. In any case, having such authority and responsibility at that young of an age would make some ponder and question. Of the wisdom behind this early responsibility is God showing the people the status and honor of the Progeny. Imam Al-Jawad (a) would stand as a testament that Muslims' connection to the Progeny was not one of emotion; rather it was based on knowledge, logic and reason. It was based on the directives of the Holy Prophet (s) and the guidance of the Holy Quran.

The person of Imam Al-Jawad (a) would be a clear proof of their faith in leadership of the Progeny after the Prophet (s). Their followers believe that one of the fundamental requirements of *imamate* is knowledge. The immaculate Imam must be the most knowledgeable individual of his time, and in fact could not be compared to anyone else in his knowledge. The knowledge of the Imam is not received through schooling, it is inherited from the Imam before him linking back to the inheritance of the knowledge of the Prophet (s). This inheritance is accorded by God's divine will.

There are no historians or books of history that criticize any of the Imams, from the Commander of the Faithful Imam Ali (a) to the last imam that people lived with and directly interacted with – Imam Al-Askari (a). On top of that, we find that history books and books specialized in studying personalities have only spoken of the Imams of the Progeny with the highest attributes of excellence, knowledge, and wisdom. Nevertheless, such acknowledgements do not necessarily prove that the Imams were the most knowledgeable of their time, nor does it prove that their knowledge was by way of divine guidance. Some may argue that indeed they were knowledgeable and wise due to the time and effort they spent in learning and studying. However, when we examine Imam Al-Jawad (a), the Ninth Imam of the Progeny, that argument cannot be made. For if time were the measure and harbor by which knowledge is received and deepened, then what time did this young imam have in which he was indisputably the most knowledgeable scholar of his era at the unassuming age of 14.

Such a miraculous feat is only possible by divine blessing and through God's will. God willed that these individuals, the Imams of the Progeny, would be the leaders of the Muslims, let alone humanity. Thus, He blessed them with their unmatched knowledge to serve as the people's guide and connection to Him after the Prophet (s). If we take some time to look back into history and examine Imam Al-Jawad's (a) lifetime, we would see his unparalleled level of knowledge that could not possibly be attained through mere study and training. This can particularly be witnessed by the different positions of both his rivals and his followers.

THE POSITION OF THE RIVALS OF THE PROGENY

When studying the relationship between the Progeny of the Prophet (s) and the ruling regimes of that time, we see that the Progeny formed the primary movement of opposition to the rulers and their regimes. Thus, it would be naturally expected that the rulers of the time, along with their followers and aides, would attempt to undermine the Progeny. History is full of futile attempts to undermine and hurt the sacred station that the Progeny held in the hearts of the people. Those attempts failed and only served to show the great attributes of the Progeny and bring people even closer to them. Imam Al-Jawad (a) was not an exception to being subject to these systematic attacks on the Progeny.

The young Al-Jawad (a), who lived within the four simple walls that formed the humble household of his father Imam Ali Al-Rida (a), would take on a tremendous task at such a young age. He was looked at as easy prey by the Abbasid regime that was resolute to sabotage the image of the Progeny (a). However, God would not accept except that Al-Jawad's (a) light were to manifest brilliantly to all those around him.

So, the Abbasids tried to undermine the young Imam and expose his "ignorance" – something they assumed would only naturally be associated with a young boy. These attempts came especially after the Abbasid Caliph Al-Ma'moun took a special interest in the young Imam. Al-Ma'moun grew very fond of Al-Jawad. Impressed by his deep wisdom, eloquent speech, and intelligent foresight, Al-Ma'moun was adamant that Al-Jawad (a) would marry his daughter Ummul Fadhl. After hearing of Al-Ma'moun's intentions, a group of his aides came to him and said, "We beg you O' Commander of the Faithful that you retreat from your decision to matter your daughter to the son of Al-Rida [Al-Jawad]. For we fear that our authority will be taken away from us and our status will be torn from us."[1] They recounted a number of reasons and interests in efforts to persuade Al-Ma'moun to change his mind regarding this issue; however, the Caliph answered them point-by-point and remained determined. He specifically said, regarding Imam Al-Jawad (a), "And of Abu Ja'far [Al-Jawad], I have chosen him for his brilliant show of knowledge surpassing all those of status despite his young age. I am impressed by him and wish for what I have seen of him to be shown to the people."

[1] Al-Mufeed, *Al-Irshad*, 2:281.

His advisors came forth with another issue. They argued that Al-Jawad (a) was still a kid who had yet to study religion and understand its laws and jurisprudence. They furthered their argument by stating that it would be best to wait some time until the boy were to engage in religious studies. Al-Ma'moun categorically rejected their argument and stated that the young Al-Jawad was more knowledgeable than they in God's Book and the tradition of the Prophet (s), in all of its details and principles. The Caliph was so confident in the Al-Jawad's (a) capability he challenged them to test to the young Imam and see for themselves. They accepted the challenge and went directly to the Yahya ibn Aktham, the Chief Judge for the Abbasid regime. The group told Aktham of the challenge thinking no one to be better than Aktham to ensure that Al-Jawad was put in his place.

Aktham planned to ask Al-Jawad a question of jurisprudence particular to the Hajj pilgrimage, given that Al-Jawad would naturally have no reason to know of the rulings of Hajj at such a young age. The gathering was organized and Aktham stood in front of the young Imam and asked, "What is the ruling on a pilgrim who has hunted?" According to Ibn Jawzi, who states that Al-Jawad was barely 8 years old at the time, the Imam (a) replied,

> *Did he hunt while in the state of* ihram *[pilgrimage] or not? Was he aware of his action or ignorant of it? Did he kill the animal purposely or by mistake? Was the pilgrim a free man or a slave? Was the pilgrim young or old? Was this the first time he hunted or not? Was the animal hunted a bird or a different type of animal? Was the animal small*

*game or large? Is the pilgrim adamant on his action or does
he regret it? Did the occurrence take place at night or in the
day? And was he in pilgrimage for* Hajj *or* Umra'*?*[2]

Ibn Aktham was baffled. He was unable to utter a word in
response to the precision in Imam Al-Jawad's (a) mere
follow-up. The astonishment on Aktham's face was clear to
all those present. Delighted Al-Ma'moun asked the Imam
(a) to answer each of the follow-up questions he asked. And
so, Al-Jawad (a) answered every element of the question and
left everyone present in awe.[3]

If the Imam (a) was not knowledgeable as he was then those
who swore enmity towards the Progeny and their followers
would have taken advantage of such a weakness. They
would have used that as an opportunity to quell the Shia
and propagate flaws in their creed. However, the Imam (a)
silenced those efforts in his brilliant display of intelligence
and knowledge. He showed them all that in those fine
moments that he was the most knowledgeable individual of
his time and the rightful leader of the Muslim nation. The
situation further proved the claim of the Shia that their
Imam is always the most knowledgeable individual of his
time.

THE GENERAL POPULACE AND THE SHIA

The stance of the general public of the Shia during the time
of Imam Al-Jawad (a) is another piece of evidence that
supports the notion that the Imam is the most

---

[2] Al-Mufeed, *Al-Irshad*, 2:282.
[3] Ibid.

knowledgeable of his time. It's important to keep historical context in mind regarding this issue. At the time of Imam Al-Jawad (a), let alone all of the Imams of the Progeny (a), being a follower of the Progeny was considered to be an unforgivable crime. Being labeled as Shia basically translated to being subject to persecution, imprisonment, torture and execution. If Imam Al-Jawad (a) did not have the same qualities of excellence and knowledge, as did the Imams before him, the followers of the Progeny would have been inclined to relinquish their faith and save themselves from such hardship. The clear divine leadership of the Imam (a) is what pushed them to hold on and sacrifice. What would be the use for these people to continue believing with all the odds against them if they were not fully convinced in the rightful leadership of the Imams?

Thus, history does not recount any instances of deviation from the path of the Progeny during the era of Imam Al-Jawad (a), or a dispute amongst the Shia on his imamate. If Al-Jawad (a) did not have the requisite knowledge it would have been only natural to see people move away from the Progeny's school of thought. This applies with all of the Imams as well. In reality, they all inherited their knowledge – young and old – from the Holy Prophet (s). The young amongst them was no different than the old. Age was not a factor. Following them was not contingent on their age, for following the young of the Progeny was just like following the old. Imam Al-Sadiq (a) who exceeded 70 years of age does not differ to us, from the aspect of creed, from Imam Al-Jawad (a) at the age of 14.

THE SHIA SCHOLARS

It is enough to simply mention one personality of the scholars of the Shia, who was also from the household of Alids[4], and his position before Imam Al-Jawad (a). Ali ibn Ja'far, the brother of Imam Moussa Al-Kadhim (a), was a dignified scholar, a narrator of the traditions of the Progeny, and a jurist whom the Progeny could rely on to help guide the people. He was a scholar in his own right, an individual whom no one could doubt or disrespect.

This man stood before the young Imam Al-Jawad (a) as a student before his teacher, a servant before his master, a follower before his leader. Even though Ali ibn Ja'far was the brother of Al-Jawad's grandfather, he would hurry to kiss the hands of the young Imam and glorify him. Those who would stand by and see Ali ibn Ja'far's humility would criticize him. Their evil spirits had no priority other than giving in to the whispers of Satan. But what a reply that ibn Ja'far would give in response to their criticism. Grabbing his white beard he would say, "If God did not qualify [me in my old age] but qualified this young man and placed him where He has, do I deny his virtue?! I beseech God from what you say, rather I am his servant."[5]

Ibn Ja'far delivers this simple yet monumental principle to us. Regardless of age, knowledge, or status, we follow the Imams because they are God's vicegerents by His decree. God honored Imam Al-Jawad (a) with his remarkable feat of knowledge and virtue at such a young age, inspiring

---

[4] Alid is a term used to refer to those who were from the lineage or bloodline of Imam Ali ibn Abi Talib (a).

[5] Al-Kulayni, *Al-Kafi*, 1:322.

generations in their firm belief in the Progeny of Muhammad (s).

BIOGRAPHICAL INFORMATION

Name: Muhammad

Title: Al-Jawad

Kunya (Agnomen): Abu Ja'far

Father: Imam Ali Al-Rida

Mother: Sabikah (or Khayzaran)

Born: Friday, 10th of Rajab 195 AH (811 AD)

Birthplace: Medina

Death: Wednesday, 29th of Dhul-Qi'dah 220 AH (835 AD)

Place of Death: Baghdad

Age at Death: 25

Gravesite: Kadhimiyan Shrine, Baghdad, Iraq

IMAM AL-HADI
Patience Against all Odds

In the Name of God, the most Beneficent, the most Merciful

*God rewarded them for their patience with a garden and
[garments of] silk, reclining therein on couches, without
facing any [scorching] sun, or [biting] cold. Its shades will
be close over them and its clusters [of fruits] will be hanging
low. They will be served around with vessels of silver and
goblets of crystal... [They will be told]: 'This is your reward,
and your efforts have been well-appreciated.'*[1]

These are the rewards that God has promised to the most
patient. In return for all that they had to endure, God
reserves the most precious rewards to his most loyal
servants. This is the position of our Holy Prophet (s) and
his Progeny of Immaculate Imams (a). Each is a role model
in his own right and each has a lifetime of immense wisdom
and grand morals that must be learned from.

Due to his circumstances, there is relatively little that we
know about Imam Ali Al-Hadi (a) and his life. But the little

---

[1] The Holy Quran. Chapter 76 [Man; Arabic: *Al-Insaan*]. Verses 12-22.

that we know shows us that he espoused the same set of virtues and noble characteristics that his forbearers had held. Chief amongst those virtues is that of patience, for which God has promised great rewards.

JOURNEY TO SAMARRA

Imam Ali Al-Hadi (a), as with most of our Immaculate Imams (a), chose to live in Medina, the city of his grandfather Prophet Muhammad (s).

But like his forefathers, Imam Al-Hadi (a) had many envious enemies in Medina. The governor of Medina, Abdullah ibn Muhammad, was especially envious of the Imam (a) and continued to harass and bother him. Abdullah ibn Muhammad also plotted to have the Imam moved away from Medina so he can act there as he pleased without any opposition.

Abdullah ibn Muhammad wrote a letter to the Abbasid caliph of the time, Al-Mutawakkil, urging him to take Imam Al-Hadi (a) to the Abbasid capital in Baghdad. That way, Mutawakkil can keep a close eye on the Imam (a) and anyone who met with him or supported him.

Knowing of the letter that Abdullah ibn Muhammad wrote to Mutawakkil, Imam Ali Al-Hadi (a) wrote a rejoinder and sent it to Baghdad, denying all the false claims that the governor had made.

Mutawakkil knew better than to show his hostility to the Imam (a). Instead, he wrote Imam Al-Hadi (a) a letter of feign praise and admiration. In the letter, Mutawakkil apologized to the Imam (a) and promised that he will remove Abdullah ibn Muhammad. Nonetheless, Mutawakkil asked the Imam (a) to make the journey the new Abbasid capital in Samarra, close to Baghdad. Mutawakkil also sent men with the letter to make sure that Imam Al-Hadi (a) did not refuse to come to Samarra. The Imam (a) obliged.[2]

The Slums

Despite his honeyed words, Mutawakkil held a great deal of animosity and envy towards our Immaculate Imam (a). Right when our Imam (a) arrived to Samarra, Mutawakkil ordered that he be quartered in the slums. Mutawakkil wanted to insult the Imam (a) and demean him. But our Imams are greater than to be demeaned simply by where they stay.

While Imam Al-Hadi (a) was staying in the slums, a companion by the name of Salih ibn Saeed came to him and complained, "They are trying so hard to dim the light [of your guidance] and demean you, until they quartered you in this slum!"

Imam Al-Hadi (a) smiled. He gestured with his hand and said, "*You are here, oh ibn Saeed!*" As ibn Saeed looked around, all he could see was the slums fading away and are replaced by heavenly gardens with flowing rivers and treasures of every kind. He was dazed in amazement at what the Imam (a) was showing him. The Imam (a) then said, "*Oh ibn Saeed! Wherever we may be, this is our [real] abode! We are not in the slums!*"[3]

---

[2] Al-Mufeed, *Al-Irshaad*, 2:309.

[3] Ibid, 2:311.

Soon after, Mutawakkil allowed the Imam (a) to move to a better neighborhood. Mutawakkil had realized that he cannot demean the Imam (a) through such ploys. Instead, Mutawakkil made sure to appear publically as though he favors the Imam (a), but all the while fought hard to deprive the Imam (a) of his following.

CONSTANT HARASSMENT

Imam Ali Al-Hadi (a) was constantly harassed by the oppressive authorities of the time. In one instance, Al-Mutawakkil, the Abbasid caliph of the time, sent one of his servants – Saeed Al-Hajib – to search the Imam's (a) house in secret. There were allegations that the Imam (a) was collecting funds and arms and preparing for a revolution against the Abbasid throne.

Saeed approached the Imam's (a) house with a ladder. He climbed to the top of the house and attempted to get in to the courtyard. However, due to the darkness of the night, he could not find his way down.

All of a sudden, he heard a man calling, *"Oh Saeed, wait until they bring you a candle."* Soon they brought him a candle and he was able to get into the house. Once inside, he saw the Imam (a) sitting on his prayer rug wearing a wool overcoat and cap. The furniture in the Imam's (a) house consisted mostly of straw mats. Saeed was struck by the Imam's (a) humble home and clothing, not to mention his welcoming demeanor towards an intruder.

The Imam (a) told Saeed to carry out his task and search the house as he was commanded. But all that Saeed could find was a large bag of coins[4] sealed with the stamp of Mutawakkil's mother, as well as another smaller pouch. The Imam then signaled to him to search the prayer area. Under the mat, Saeed found a sword in a worn out sheath. Saeed took the bags of coins and the sword and head back to the caliph's castle.

When Mutawakkil saw his mother's stamp on the bag of coins, he called her to his court and inquired about why that might be at Imam Al-Hadi's (a) home. She explained to him that, a while back, when Mutawakkil had fallen gravely ill, she had made an oath to God that if he is cured she would grant a large amount of money to Imam Ali ibn Muhammad (a). Mutawwakil had actually fallen so gravely ill that his family feared it were his last days on earth. The doctors could not seem to find what his illness was or how to cure it. Eventually, Mutawakkil had written to Imam Hadi (a) asking him if he could find him a cure. It was through Imam Hadi's (a) medicine that Mutawakkil regained his health. And when he did, his mother made good on her oath and sent the money to the Imam (a). Yet despite the enormous wealth that she had sent him, the Imam (a) did not even take off the seal to count or use the money.

Mutawkkil then turned to the smaller pouch and opened it. It had a meager 400 dinars – nowhere near what it would take to raise an army and sustain a revolution. When Mutawakkil saw this, he became at ease and knew that rumors of revolt could not be further away from the truth.

---

[4] A specific name, 'Badra,' is given to the type of bag that was used. Historians disagree how much such a pouch would carry, with some say that it would be around 10,000 dinars – a relatively large amount of cash.

He gave Saeed the sword and pouch of coins, and added another bag of coins like the one his mother had given. He commanded to go back to the Imam (a) and give him back his belongings.[5]

This was not the only time that Mutawakkil or the other Abbasid caliph would harass Imam Al-Hadi (a). In fact, there are many separate and distinct stories of the caliph sending men to search the home of our Tenth Immacualte Imam (a). As they had done with all of our other Imams (a), the rulers of the time continued to harm and harass our Immaculate Guides (a). Yet the Imams (a) continued in patience and perseverance.

MUTAWAKKIL'S REIGN

Yet Mutawakkil had an especially malign attitude towards the Progeny of the Prophet (s). He continued to harass the grandchildren of the Commander of the Faithful (a) and Lady Fatima (a). He went so far as to transgress against the shrine of Imam Hussain (a) and its visitors.

Mutawakkil held so much hatred for the Progeny of the Prophet (s) that he tried to eviscerate the land of Karbala from all marks and monuments that reminded the people of the stance of Imam Hussain (a) in that land. He commanded his men to tear down the edifice that was built over the holy graves and attempted to remove all signs of the grave by turning the land into a farm. But as the farmers attempted to run their oxen over the holy land, the animals would refuse to trample over the grave. It wasn't long after

---

[5] Al-Qummi, *Muntaha Al-Aamaal*, 2:497-98.

these crimes that Mutawakkil was killed by his own son who sought the throne for himself.

Imam Ali Al-Hadi (a) had to live through the reign of such tyrants, as his forefathers had done before him. He was patient and persevered until he was martyred by poison at the hands of the Abbasids.

IMAM AL-HADI'S (A) MARTYRDOM

Our scholars narrate that Imam Ali Al-Hadi (a) was poisoned by Mu'tamid, the brother of the Abbasid caliph at the time Mu'tazz. But even on his deathbed, our Tenth Immaculate Imam (a) did not stop the flow of his wisdom and blessings to his followers.

During the last days of his life, the Imam (a) was being visited by some of his followers. He would tell one of them, whose name was Abu Du'ama, "*Oh Abu Du'ama! I am obliged to you now [because of your visit]. Shall I not relate to you something that will please you?*" Abu Du'ama asked the Imam (a) to continue. Imam Hadi (a) said,

> *My father, Muhammad ibn Ali, said – relating from his father Ali, from his father Musa ibn Jafaar, from his father Jafaar ibn Muhammad, from his father Muhammad ibn Ali, from his father Ali ibn Al-Husayn, from his father Al-Husayn ibn Ali, from his father Ali ibn Abi Talib, may God send his blessings upon them all – that the Prophet (s) told Ali (a), 'Write, oh Ali.' [Imam Ali (a)] asked, 'What should I write?' The Prophet (s) said, 'Write: In the Name of God the Most Beneficent, the Most Merciful. Faith is what has been preserved in the hearts and*

corroborated by deeds. Islam is what is spoken by the tongue...'

Abu Du'ama exclaimed in amazement, "Oh Grandson of the Prophet (s)! I don't know which is more brilliant, the narration or its chain of narrators!" The Imam (a) replied, *"It is surely written on a parchment in the handwriting of Ali ibn Abi Talib (a) as relayed to him by the Prophet (s), and it has been passed amongst us [Immaculate Imams] through the generations."*[6]

Abu Du'ama was right to be amazed by the Imam's (a) words. Such narrations especially highlight the reasons why we follow this line of leaders. Not only is their knowledge so immense, but their connection with the divine is ever so clear. They are the Progeny of the Prophet (s). They are the Household of Purity. They are the keepers of the Prophet's (s) knowledge and wisdom. They are the inheritors of all prophets passed.

And who else can boast a relation to the divine like theirs?

---

[6] Al-Qummi, *Muntaha Al-Aamaal*, 2:503.

BIOGRAPHICAL INFORMATION

Name: Ali

Title: Al-Hadi

Kunya (Agnomen): Abul-Hassan

Father: Imam Muhammad Al-Jawad

Mother: Sumanah

Born: Friday, 2nd of Rajab, 212 AH (827 AD)

Birthplace: Surya (suburb of Medina)

Died: Monday, 26th of Jumadil-Thani 254 AH (868 AD)

Place of Death: Samarra

Age at Death: 42

Gravesite: Al-Askari Shrine, Samarra, Iraq

IMAM AL-ASKARI
The Progeny's Honor and Nobility

In the Name of God, the most Beneficent, the most Merciful

Indeed God chose Adam and Noah, and the progeny of Abraham and the progeny of Imran above all the nations; some of them are descendants of the others, and God is all-hearing, all-knowing.[1]

Writing, reading, remembering, and learning about Imam Hassan Al-Askari (a) is a unique task as it relates directly to the Imam of Our Time – Imam Al-Mahdi (a). Imam Al-Askari (a) is our living Imam's (a) father. And thus naturally, this relationship strikes a particular core with our living Imam (a) as his father lived and died to protect him as the last heir and successor of the Progeny (a).

In this particular chapter, though brief in nature, I wish to shed some light on the life of this immaculate individual as I have done with his fathers before him. The role Imam Al-Askari (a) played and the effect he had on the nation was profound. I would like to showcase a flower from every

---

[1] The Holy Quran. Chapter 3 [Family of Imran; Arabic: *Aal Imran*]. Verse 33-34.

orchard of his and a branch from some of its trees, because more than that I could not possibly do as the orchards of Al-Askari (a) reach far beyond the eye can see.

THE CIRCUMSTANCES HE LIVED IN

Imam Al-Askari (a) was called Abu Muhammad and also known as Ibn Al-Rida. He was born on the 8th of Rabee' Al-Thani in the year 232 AH in the Holy City of Medina. He only lived until 28 years of age, killed by poison like his fathers before him.[2] And though his life was short, he endured several lifetimes' worth of pain, sorrow, and suffering. He accompanied his father Imam Ali Al-Hadi (a) from Medina to Samarra as his father was summoned by the Abbasid caliph Al-Mutawakkil to remain under his watchful eye in Iraq. Essentially, the Imam (a) was placed under house arrest in his move to Samarra. Imam Al-Askari (a) witnessed all the discomfort his father endured, being monitored and watched over as if he were a criminal. When his father was killed, Imam Al-Askari (a) assumed the active role of imamate at the age of 22. He took on the responsibility fully with all its challenges and hardships, considering that it was no less difficult than during his father's era.

What are the reasons for the Abbasids continued and focused effort to suppress the descendants of the Holy Prophet (s)? Reason would follow that the Abbasids would be more lenient towards the Progeny (a) given the fact that the Imams (a) clearly showed that their focus was on

---

[2] Al-Tabrasi, *I'laam Al-Waraa*, 2:131.

developing the community's intellectual and spiritual dimensions. The Imams (a) did not participate in any of the revolts of rebellions that made way against the caliphate. Moreover, from a political standpoint it made sense that the Abbasids would rule with an iron fist during the advent of their caliphate since they had the interest of establishing their uncontested authority before the people. However, why would they continue to suppress after so many years of establishing their dominion and control over the state? There are a number of reasons for this:

For one, the Progeny (a) had a special place in the hearts and souls of the community and that is something the Abbasids knew very well. One year, The Abbasid caliph Haroun Al-Rashid went to Mecca for hajj. He saw Imam Al-Kadhim (a) at the Ka'ba and decided to go up to him. He said, "So you're the one people pay allegiance to in secret?" To that Imam Al-Kadhim (a) replied, "*I am the leader of the hearts and you are the leader of the bodies.*"[3] This special connection between the Imam (a) and the people worried the Abbasids causing them unease of how influential these Imams (a) would be over the people.

The Abbasids were the closest people to the Progeny (a) and in fact, before they ascended the caliphate, they were considered to be amongst the *Shia* (followers) of the Progeny (a). They knew fully of the idea of imamate and that it ended with the Awaited Imam Al-Mahdi (a), who would be a direct threat to their seat of power because he would have the divine task of establishing peace and justice

[3] Al-Mar'ashi Al-Najafi, *Sharh Thqaq Al-Haqq*, 19:548. Citing: Allama Sheikh Yaseen ibn Ibrahim Al-Nahouti Al-Shaafa'i, *Al-Anwar Al-Qudsiya*, 38.

on God's Earth. It is from this point that the Abbasids placed an even higher priority to isolate the Imams (a) especially with Imam Al-Askari (a) and his father in putting them under house arrest in Samarra. The authorities did this to keep a close eye on the family and wait until the Mahdi (a) was born. They even employed women to visit the home and report back to the Abbasids to give any news of the Imam's (a) wife being pregnant with a child. The Abbasids thought that by utilizing such methods they could preempt the divine will that would be manifested with the birth and rise of Imam Al-Mahdi (a).

After the death of Imam Al-Askari (a) they stormed his house to confirm the rumor that the Mahdi (a) was born. Sheikh Al-Mufeed describes the situation saying,

> ... the Imam left his son, the Awaited One for the state of justice, and concealed his birth due to the difficult times they faced. The ruler of the time inquired too inquisitively into his presence. The Imam (a) did not allow anyone to know of the Mahdi's (a) birth when he was alive nor did the masses know of it after the Imam's (a) death...[4]

Al-Rawandi writes in his book Al-Khara'ij, "Ja'far Al-Kathab – 'the Liar' – came to the Abbasid Al-Mu'tamad and revealed to him of the presence of the Mahdi (a). Thereafter, Al-Mu'tamad went with his guards and captured the Mahdi's (a) mother – Sayqal – and demanded that she give up her child. She denied their accusations...["][5] Some chaos arose in the city of Basra which seamlessly diverted

4 Al-Mufeed, Al-Irshad, 2:336.
5 Al-Rawandi, Al-Khara'ij wal-Jarayih, 3:110.

their attention away from Sayqal, and by God's grace she was saved from their hands.

THE MOST IMPORTANT QUALITIES

There were so many outstanding qualities and features of Imam Al-Askari (a) that made him stand out as an individual generally and a leader specifically. Through the positions he took, the priorities he had, and commitment to principle he played the core role in protecting the Shi'ism and Shia. This aspect of the discussion can be split into a couple major points.

The Personality of the Imam (a)

With all of the challenges and difficulties that Imam Al-Askari (a) faced at such a young age and the short life that he lived, he was able to assert himself in a society that had all the odds stacked against him. He affirmed his presence with the people even though most opposed him and did not follow him. He did not succumb to the whims of the oppressors nor did he subjugate himself as inferior to the general opposition held by the authorities and the masses. Ahmad ibn Ubaydallah ibn Al-Khaqan, praised Imam Al-Askari (a) and described him in much detail. This particular scholar was not a follower of the Progeny (a) and was in fact considered to be very much opposed to them in his belief. He said,

> I have never seen nor have I known a man like Al-Hassan ibn Ali ibn Muhammad ibn Ali Al-Rida with such composure, tranquility, humbleness, honor, nobility, and prestige from amongst the Progeny and the entirety of Banu

*Hashim. His presence at such a young age was impressive
and he was held in such high esteem by leaders, ministers,
and the masses. I remember I was at the service of my father
when he had a gathering of people. One of the house servants
came to my father and said, 'Abu Muhammad – ibn Al-
Rida – is on the door.' My father responded in a loud voice,
'Let him in.' I was quite surprised that the courtiers had
the nerve to honor someone with a nickname as such in my
father's presence – that was an honor reserved only to the
caliph, the caliph's successor, or for an honorary title given
by the order of the caliph. So a young, handsome, tall, solid-
looking man of tan complexion and great posture walks in.
He had a prestige and aura about him. When he came in,
my father got up from his seat and walked towards him –
which I have never seen him do for anyone from Banu
Hashim or the leadership. My father embraced him, kissed
him, and sat him right next to him. As my father praised
him and welcomed him, I stared in astonishment... Later
on I came by and found my father praying. I waited until he
finished. As he completed his prayers he turned to me and
asked, 'Do you need something Ahmad?' I replied, 'Yes
father, if you give me permission I will ask you.' He told
me, 'Go ahead.' So I asked my father, 'Who was that man
that you welcomed in such a way, praising him, admiring
him, and even telling him that you would sacrifice yourself
for him?' He answered, 'My son, that is the Imam of the
Rafida[6], Al-Hassan ibn Ali, who is known as Ibn Al-
Rida.' He paused for a moment, and I did the same and*

---

[6] Rafida was a term used to describe the Shia – the followers of the Progeny.
Rafida literally means rejectors and was a reference to describe the Shia as the
group that rejected the caliphs other than Imam Ali (a).

did not speak. He then said, 'My son, if the imamate were to be removed from our caliphs of Banu Abbas no one would deserve it from Banu Hashim but him. This is for his virtue, humbleness, guidance, insight, asceticism, worship, beautiful ethics, and goodness. And if you were to see his father you would see a noble, virtuous, and honorable man.' I only became more worried about my father and grew angry with him. I kept thinking about it. All I could think of and all I could do was ask around about this man my father adored. Everywhere I asked from writers, jurists, leaders, judges, and all other people, I could not find a single soul that would not praise him for his greatness. He was described with the best of praise, the highest of attributes and the finest of words... his value grew in my eyes as I saw that no friend or enemy could say anything but the best of things about him.[7]

His Role in Protecting Islam and the Intellectual Heritage of the Progeny

The harsh circumstances that Imam Al-Askari (a) lived through were not conducive to an environment for teaching the sciences that his forefathers had taught, like Imams Al-Baqir (a), Al-Sadiq (a), and Al-Kadhim (a). Imam Al-Askari (a) was under immense pressure, being virtually choked by the authorities at his every move. Remember, he was not living in Medina – he was under the caliphate's surveillance in the military town of Samarra. Unlike Medina and Baghdad, which had their weight as cities of research and science, Samarra was basically a barracks city with a heavy presence of the Abbasid military. So the Imam (a) was

---

[7] Al-Mufeed, *Al-Irshad*, 2:321-23.

robbed the opportunity to engage people and teach in the manner that his grandfathers did. Nevertheless, he still emanated the light of Muhammad (s) through any people he did encounter.

There are countless scholars who narrated from him. In fact, there is a book called "Tafseer Al-Imam Al-Askari" which is a book of Quranic exegesis that was attributed to the Imam (a). Though there are disagreements over this book being properly attributed to the Imam (a) that does not prevent the presence of numerous narrations in this book that are from him. This is in addition to the various bold stances the Imam (a) took to defend the faith, its principles, and the proper creed taught by the Holy Prophet (s). In one situation, the Imam (a) stumped the esteemed philosopher known as Al-Kindi, who tried to argue that the Quran contradicted itself. Al-Kindi published a book about the supposed contradictions in the Quran and busied himself with that work. One of Al-Kindi's students – who happened to be an assigned house servant at the house the Imam (a) was placed in Samarra – entered the Imam's (a) house.

Imam Al-Askari (a) asked him, "*Is there not a guided man amongst you to oppose your teacher Al-Kindi in what he has taken up with the Quran?*" He replied to the Imam (a), "We are his students. How could we oppose him in this matter or in any other?" The Imam (a) then said, "*Will you tell him what I give you?*" He said, "Yes." The Imam (a) said,

> *Go to him and get closer to him through your helpfulness and kindness, aiding him in his work. If the subject is brought up then say to him, 'There is something that has*

come to mind regarding this matter that I wish to ask you about.' He will accept your question. Then say, 'If the speaker of this Quran came to you, would it possible that his intention in what he says is different than the meanings that you have presumed and taken?' He will answer, 'That is possible,' because he is a man who comprehends if he listens. When he answers that way then say, 'So how can you be sure that he intended what you have presumed and not instead placed a different meaning from what is seemingly apparent?'[8]

So, the student went to Al-Kindi and when the issue came up he spoke to his teacher in the exact manner that the Imam (a) instructed him. After hearing what he had to say Al-Kindi said, "Repeat it to me again." He then thought to himself and found the great plausibility of the argument both linguistically and theoretically. He turned to his student again and said, "Tell me where you got this argument from." The student replied, "Nowhere. It was something that I thought of so I presented it to you." Al-Kindi told him, "No. Someone like you won't come to something like this, nor would anyone from this place. So tell me where did you got this from?" The student said, "Abu Muhammad instructed me with this." Al-Kindi replied, "Now you have come with truth. An answer like that would not come except from that house." Then Al-Kindi ordered for a fire to be made, took his book and burned it in its flames.[9]

This particular story should not be looked at lightly. The Holy Quran is the greatest source of Islamic thought. When

[8] Ibn Shahr Ashoob, *Manaqib Aal Abi Talib*, 3:525-26.
[9] Ibid.

it is being doubted and argued about as a contradiction –
that is a grave danger to the intellectual and spiritual
foundations of the Muslim community. Especially when
such arguments come from renowned Muslim philosophers,
the danger of doubt caused is very serious. Not addressing
such issues will have an immediate impact on society as well
as long-term impacts with the generations that come later.
Notice that in addressing this issue with Al-Kindi the Imam
(a) did not deal with him by calling him a heretic and
disrespecting him. Rather, the Imam (a) dealt with the
situation in such a creative and wise way – creativity and
finesse that is characteristic of the Progeny (a). The Imams
(a) rebutted ideological deviance with evidence and proof
not with loudness and vulgarity. They presented intellectual
arguments as opposed to accusing others of heresy out of
ignorance, waging wars, shedding blood, and making others
out to be disbelievers. This is what distinguishes the
Progeny (a) and their students from others, they do not
utilize *takfir*[10] like other groups. Instead, they address
deviance as God ordered, *"Invite to the way of your Lord with
wisdom and good advice and dispute with them in a manner that is
best…"*[11]

These are only some basic points that the Imam (a)
provided for us in his short life. He played a monumental
role in preparing the community and foreshadowing the
occultation of his son Imam Al-Mahdi (a). This particular
area requires much more depth, further research, and longer

---

[10] Takfir is an Arabic term referring to the act of making others out to be
disbelievers and heretics. This method was characteristically used by the
Kharajites and continued to be used between warring factions in Islamic history.
[11] The Holy Quran. Chapter 16 [The Bees; Arabic: *Al-Nahl*]. Verse 125.

discussions. I will touch on this in the next chapter and encourage the reader to nonetheless look even deeper in this regard, as it relates to each and every one of us living today.

BIOGRAPHICAL INFORMATION

Name: Hassan

Title: Al-Askari

Kunya (Agnomen): Abu Muhammad

Father: Imam Ali Al-Hadi

Mother: Haditha (also referred to as Susan)

Born: Friday, 8th Rabi'ul-Thani 232 AH (847 AD)

Birthplace: Medina

Died: Friday, 8th of Rabi'ul-Awwal 260 AH (874 AD)

Place of Death: Samarra

Age at Death: 28

Gravesite: Al-Askari Shrine, Samarra, Iraq

IMAM AL-MAHDI
Awaiting the Reappearance

In the Name of God, the most Beneficent, the most Merciful

God has promised those of you who have faith and do righteous deeds that He will surely make them successors in the earth, just as He made those who were before them successors, and He will surely establish for them their religion which He has approved for them, and that He will surely change their state to security after their fear, while they worship Me, not ascribing any partners to Me. Whoever is ungrateful after that—it is they who are the transgressors.[1]

It is narrated that our Fourth Immaculate Imam, Imam Ali Zayn Al-Abideen (a), would read this verse and say,

By God! These are our followers. They will be lead to this by a man from amongst us [the Progeny of the Holy Prophet (s)] – the Mahdi of this nation. He is the one whom the Messenger of God (s) described saying, 'If there were only one day left on this earth, God would extend that

---

[1] The Holy Quran. Chapter 24 [The Light; Arabic: *Al-Noor*]. Verse 55.

day until a man of my Progeny appears and whose name is my name. He will fill the earth with justice and equity after it was filled with oppression and inequity.[2]

Similar narrations have been passed down from Imam Baqir and Imam Sadiq.[3]

God has promised us a day when an Immaculate Imam from the Progeny of our Holy Prophet (s) will come and bring peace and justice to a world filled with strife and injustice. On such a day, God's promise will be fulfilled and relief from injustice and inequity will be delivered at the hands of our Promised Mahdi (a).

Speaking of our Twelfth Immaculate Imam (a) – his life, his movement, his occultation, and his reappearance – is a long and worth endeavor. There have been many books and much research written, tackling distinct aspects of this study. We will attempt to shed light on one aspect of our relationship with our Imam (a) for this short treatise – namely, our responsibility during the time of the Occultation.

WHAT IS THE REQUIRED STANCE OF A PERSON IN THE TIME OF OCCULTATION?

Amongst the narrations of Ahlulbayt (a), there are some narrations that are better known than others. These narrations are characteristic in describing awaiting 'the relief' – the reappearance of the Imam (a).

2 Al-Huwaizi, *Tafseer Noor Al-Thaqalayn*, 3:62.
3 Ibid.

The Commander of the Faithful (a) said, "*Await the relief and do not lose hope in God, for the dearest act to God is awaiting the relief.*"[4] It is also narrated that when Imam Al-Sadiq (a) was listing the characteristics of true faith he said, "*Devotion, chastity, righteousness... and awaiting the relief with patience.*"[5]

We can interpret 'awaiting the relief' or 'awaiting the reappearance' in two ways:

The first view holds that, in the era of occultation, we are not to engage in anything that is incompatible with waiting, whether it be engaging in the good or forbidding the evil. Nor should we initiate any social change that is aimed at bringing reform for the community or the nation. Some people in this camp go to the extent to believe and propagate the necessity of spreading corruption, because in their twisted belief the more corruption spreads in the world the faster the reappearance will come. They believe that the Imam (a) will not reappear except by the Earth being completely plagued by corruption and immorality.

Even though some hold this view, this outlook on 'awaiting the relief' is perverse, erroneous, and the farthest possible perspective on what it truly means to await the reappearance.

The second view holds that, in awaiting the Imam (a), we are supposed to ready ourselves and prepare for his arrival and the day that has been promised by God. In anticipation of a guest or a relative that will be paying a visit to your house, do you not make sure that every aspect of the home

---

[4] Al-Sadr, *Tareekh Al-Ghayba Al-Kubra*, 321.
[5] Ibid.

is prepared so that you can welcome your guest in the proper way? Naturally, we make sure that the house is clean, the dishes are washed, there is food and drink to offer the guest, and that the house is a place that our guest will feel welcome in. You take care of these preparations before your guest arrives, not when they knock on the door. How embarrassed would we be if a visitor were to knock, knowing that they would come at any time, but did not make an effort to prepare for their arrival? In the same way, waiting for the Imam (a) requires us to prepare for his arrival so that when he does arrive we are able to serve him and properly join him.

The Imam (a) will come at a time known to no other but God. It is narrated that someone asked the Holy Prophet (s), "O' Messenger of God, when will the savior from your progeny rise?" The Prophet (s) would respond, *"His [situation regarding the time of his rise] is analogous to the [situation regarding the] Time [of the Day of Judgment]. Only God knows when it will be..."*[6] Therefore, we must make our most diligent effort to prepare for him in every possible moment of our lives. If we do not, we are likely to be caught off guard and even shocked by the Imam's (a) reappearance.

GETTING TO KNOW THE IMAM

A person must, first and foremost, prepare himself for the reappearance of the Imam (a) mentally and psychologically. This comes only through believing in the Imam (a) and understanding his role and message. We must try to get to

---

[6] Al-Khazzaz Al-Qummi, *Kifayet Al-Athar*, 277.

know our living Imam (a) – the more we get to know him, the closer we become to him and the better prepared we become for his reappearance.

And in order to get to know the Imam (a), we must study his person, his position, and his role.

His Person

We must seek to know who our living Imam (a) is. We know that he is the son of our Eleventh Immaculate, Imam Hassan Al-Askari (a), and that he was born in the year 255 after Hijra (869 CE). But we must seek to know more and more about his holy personality.

It is this knowledge of the Imam's (a) holy person that has safeguarded the followers of the Ahlulbayt from falling into the traps of misguidance. We see that in other schools of thought, people were misguided by men who claimed to be the promised savior. But the phenomena are much less prevalent in Shia Islam. That is because the followers of the Ahlulbayt know that their Twelfth Immaculate Imam is Imam Muhammad Al-Mahdi (a) the son of Imam Hassan Al-Askari (a). It is difficult for anyone to claim that he is the son of the Imam born 1200 years ago. Thus knowledge of who our Imam (a) is has saved us from such misguidance.

His Position

We must seek to understand what the position of our Imam Mahdi (a) is. What does it mean that he is the *Imam*? What does it mean that he is *Immaculate*?

We must know that he is the Immaculate – that he, out of his own free will, has chosen to distance himself from all sin and be the closest creation to God Almighty. We must know that he has been given by God the position of Imam over all Muslims. Thus, we must bear allegiance to him and follow him in all his directives. God Almighty says in his Holy Book,

> *O you who have faith! Obey God and obey the Apostle and those vested with authority among you. And if you dispute concerning anything, refer it to God and the Apostle, if you have faith in God and the Last Day. That is better and more favorable in outcome.*[7]

Our Twelfth Immaculate Imam (a) is the one whom God has vested this authority.

Our relationship to the Immaculate Imam (a) – the Master of our Time – cannot be like our relationship to any other leader. We may follow other leaders to find that they are fallible individual. They make mistakes and fall in error.

But our relationship to our Imam (a) is much different. He is the Immaculate Imam (a) as appointed by God Almighty. There is no room for error when God's representative and proof on earth is at the helm. If we know this about our Imam (a), then we know that the promised day of justice and equity is inevitable – our relationship to the Imam (a) becomes much stronger with that knowledge.

If we know that our Imam (a) is the manifestation of God's guidance, our relationship with our Imam (a) becomes that much stronger.

This is why Imam Sadiq (a) taught us to repeat this supplication during the time of the occultation,

---

[7] The Holy Quran. Chapter 4 [The Women; Arabic: *Al-Nisaa*]. Verse 59.

Oh God, grant me knowledge of Your Self, for if you did not grant me knowledge of Your Self, I would not know Your Prophet (s). Oh God, grant me knowledge of Your Prophet (s), for if you did not grant me knowledge of Your Prophet (s), I would not know Your Proof [i.e. the Immaculate Imam] (a). Oh God, grant me knowledge of Your Proof (a), for if you did not grant me knowledge of Your Proof (a), I would surely become misguided in my faith.[8]

His Role

We cannot truly be 'waiting' for the Imam (a) if we do not understand his role now and his role after the end of the occultation.

Even during the occultation, he has an active and direct role in our lives. As followers of the Ahlulbayt, the Imam (a) is our master and our guardian. Even when we do not interact with him and do not perceive his direct impact on our world, he continues to be a source of mercy and blessings.

In one signed letter that our Twelfth Holy Imam (a) sent to Sheikh Mufeed, he said,

We are in a place away from the lands of the oppressors, as God has shown us the great benefit to us and our followers [from this occultation] so long as the world remains in the hands of the wretched. Yet we are still privy to your news. There is nothing about you that we do not know. We are not neglectful towards you. Neither have we forgotten you. If it were not [for our remembrance of you], you would have

---

8 Al-Kulayni, *Al-Kafi*, 1:337.

been in a greater difficulty and would have been exterminated by your enemy.[9]

PRACTICAL WAYS TO PREPARE FOR THE IMAM (A)

What are the essential methods and ways that we can follow whereby we are considered as people awaiting the Imam (a) and preparing for his reappearance?

Adhering to the Line of the Great Maraji' (Jurists)

God's wisdom dictated that He would guide people and counsel them to the true righteous path by sending prophets and messengers. After the prophets and the messengers God sent vicegerents as the leaders of truth guiding people to His path. The vicegerents take people by the hand and lead them to their Lord. Sometimes people see how the vicegerents exercise their role, and at other times the role of the vicegerents – albeit present and necessary – is covert or hidden from the people. In the era of occultation (when the Imam's identity is hidden), this same proof of God must exist. There must be someone who bears this proof upon the people and is ready to clarify to them what their obligations and duties are. God can provide such an individual and because He is so Kind, He definitely does provide such an individual. But because of the problems people make, in order to protect this vicegerent or for other possible wisdoms, God may command the vicegerent to keep his identity hidden from people in certain circumstances. In such circumstances, the Imam (a) continues to play his role to the greatest extent possible.

---

[9] Al-Tabrasi, *Al-Ihtijaj*, 2:323.

The Imam (a) made the scholars the proof upon people so that we may follow them in his absence. They are his proof upon the people and he, the Imam (a), is God's proof. *"In your current affairs go back to the narrators of our traditions [i.e. the jurists], for they are my proof upon you and I am God's proof."*[10] In regards to the jurists and their authority, it is narrated that Imam Al-Sadiq (a) said,

> ... *Let them be content with them as judges, for I have made them an authority over you. So if they rule in accordance to our rule, and people do not accept their verdict then the people are belittling the verdict of God. In that, they dispute our authority, and those who dispute our authority dispute the authority of God – and that is equal to ascribing a partner to God.*[11]

It is essential that we emphasize the importance of choosing our *Marja'* (jurist to follow) properly. Our decision should not be based on emotion or whim. This issue is not arbitrary for a person to choose based on what appeals to them. Rather, there is a set of qualifications that a person must look at like knowledge, justice, credentials, and other matters that are listed as the requirements of being a *Marja'*. To have nationalism, love, hatred, ethnocentrism or any other affiliation be considered in one's decision of who to follow when someone else is more qualified, that is completely unacceptable. In such a case, a person's actions risk being null and void! The likes of such a situation is analogous to the state of those who would only accept from their prophets the things that they liked. When a prophet

---

[10] Al-Tousi, *Al-Ghayba*, 176; Al-Amili, *Wasael Al-Shia*, 18:101.

[11] Al-Amili, *Wasael Al-Shia*, 18:98.

was not in line with their whims, they rejected and
sometimes even killed their prophets:

> *And most certainly We gave Musa the Book and We sent
> apostles after him one after another; and We gave Isa, the
> son of Mariam, clear arguments and strengthened him with
> the holy spirit, What! whenever then an apostle came to you
> with that which your souls did not desire, you were insolent
> so you called some liars and some you slew.*[12]

Thus, it is not a legitimate excuse for a person who has
learned of the requirements of following a jurist to choose
not to follow simply because they don't 'connect' with the
jurist. In other words, you should not follow a jurist because
he fits within your political, social or economic ideology. If
we cannot follow our jurists because we are unable to shift
from our fallible preconceived notions, habits, or already
established outlooks, then how do we expect to follow our
Imam (a) once he reappears? The Imam (a) will come to
elevate humanity above invalid traditions, customs, and
beliefs. He will bring reform to what many have held to be
part and parcel of their ideologies and worldviews. The
inability to follow a jurist based on the proper qualifications
and prerequisites will result in a greater likelihood of
deviance when the Awaited Imam (a) reappears.

Building Our Spirituality and Creed

Preparing for the reappearance of the Imam (a) requires us
to develop ourselves spiritually and theologically. The Imam
(a) needs supporters who are strong in their creed, ethics,

---

[12] The Holy Quran. Chapter 2 [The Cow; Arabic: *Al-Baqara*]. Verse 87.

and abilities that can only be fortified by building one's spirituality through learning the teachings of the religion.

The noble narrations describe this group of supporters for Imam Al-Mahdi (a). There is a specific narration from Imam Hussain (a) regarding the Mahdi (a) that says,

> *The people of the era of the [Mahdi's] occultation who believe in his leadership and await his reappearance are better than the people of any era. This is because God gave them intellect, understanding, and knowledge that caused the occultation to be for them as if they see [the Imam]. And God made the people of that era at the status of the warriors of the Holy Prophet (s). They are truly the sincere ones... and call to [the way of] God in secret and in the open.*[13]

Sheikh Al-Tousi also narrates that the Holy Prophet (s) said, "*There will be a people after you, that one of their men's reward [for his deeds] will be worth the reward for fifty of your men.*" Those around him replied, "O' Messenger of God, we were with you in the Battles of Badr, Uhud, Hunayn, and the Quran was revealed to us..." The Prophet (s) then said, "*If you were to bear what they bear, you would not have their patience.*"[14]

True preparation translates into a person feeling a greater responsibility in the era of occultation to build a strong righteous community. It means that we engage in the good and forbid the evil. It means that we discipline, develop and advance ourselves in our creed and ethics. By being in this mindset and state of living, it will help us better receive the

---

[13] Al-Sadr, *Tareekh Al-Ghayba Al-Kubra*, 377. Citing, Al-Sadouq, *Ikmal al-Din*, 32.
[14] Ibid.

vast changes and reform the Imam (a) will make when he reappears. Our narrations tell us that the great social and ideological reforms that the Imam (a) will bring forth will not be readily accepted by those who are not firm in their faith in God. Like the era of occultation, the era of reappearance will also witness instigation and sedition. Thus, only the ones that absorbed deeply into their religion and their true faith in God will overcome such challenges, understand the reforms of the Imam (a) and support him in his movement.

A person who is weak spiritually and theologically is less likely to accept the actions of the Imam (a) and may actually begin to doubt his leadership when he does reappear. That is why it is essential to develop one's spirituality and understanding in creed, because it makes an individual strong in facing the hardships, challenges, and ridicule during the time of occultation. Those who have not developed such a foundation may be weak and prone to lose hope in the Imam (a). Such a person may even doubt the reappearance of the Imam (a) and misconceptions may begin to take a toll on his heart.

Not Being Tied Down to this World and Material Attachments

To be effective in preparing for the Imam (a), we need to avoid being attached to the world and materialism. These things could be a cause for our drift from the cause of the Imam (a). He will come to create the greatest reform witnessed by mankind – we need to be ready to support that with all our time and resources. Having unhealthy attachments to money, entertainment, family, children, and affluence are obstacles in joining the Imam's (a) movement.

This is a reality that people before us have faced, and the Holy Quran discusses it in the following verse:

O you who believe! What (excuse) have you that when it is said to you: Go forth in God's way, you should incline heavily to earth; are you contented with this world's life instead of the hereafter? But the provision of this world's life compared with the hereafter is but little.[15]

The more things we are unhealthily attached to in this material world, the more difficult sacrifice will be. A person could be prevented from following the Imam (a) because of his inability to sacrifice what he has become deeply attached to. Our attachments could be the reason for us even standing against the Imam (a). What would be our position if the Imam (a) told us to give up our wealth because we don't have a right to it? Or what if he were to tell us to disown some of the people that are dear to us because they are not on the path of truth? What would we do if he ordered us to practice something that we felt was to difficult in following his orders? Think of your attachments and see how they could possibly be a cause for your lack of subordination for the Imam (a). To be disobedient to the immaculate Imam (a) is to be disobedient to the Prophet (s) and to God Almighty Himself.

---

[15] The Holy Quran. Chapter 9 [The Repentance; Arabic: *Al-Tawba*]. Verse 38.

BIOGRAPHICAL INFORMATION

Name: Muhammad

Title: Al-Mahdi

Kunya (Agnomen): Abul-Qassim

Father: Imam Hassan Al-Askari

Mother: Sayqal (also referred to as Narjis)

Born: Friday, 15th of Sha'ban 255 AH (869 AD)

Birthplace: Samarra

Minor Occultation: 8th of Rabi'ul-Awwal 260xAH (874 AD)

Major Occultation: 10th of Shawwal 329 AH (941 AD)

BIBLIOGRAPHY

RELIGIOUS SCRIPTURE

The Holy Quran

OTHER SOURCES

Abdul Hameed, Sa'ib. *Tareekh Al-Islam Al-Thaqafi wal-Siyasi.* Markaz Al-Ghadeer, 1997.

Al-'Ayashi, Muhammad ibn Masood. *Tafseer Al-'Ayashi.* Tehran: Al-Maktaba Al-Ilmiyya Al-Islamiyya.

Al-Adeeb, Aadil. *Al-A'imma Al-Ithna 'Ashr.* Beirut: Al-Daar Al-Islamiyya, 1979.

Al-Ahsa'i, Muhammad ibn Ali. *'Awali Al-La'ali.* Qum: Sayyid Al-Shuhada, 1983.

Al-Ameen, Muhsen. *Aa'yan Al-Shia.* 5th ed. Beirut: Daar Al-Taaruf.

Al-Amili, Muhammad ibn Al-Hassan. *Wasael Al-Shia.* Beirut: Daar Ihya Al-Torath Al-Arabi.

Al-Barqi, Ahmad ibn Muhammad. *Al-Mahasin.* Tehran: Daar Al-Kutub Al-Islamiya, 1950.

Al-Hakeem, Muhammad Baqir. *Al-Zahraa: Sermons and Discussions of Shaheed Al-Mihrab Ayatullah Sayyid Muhammad Baqir Al-Hakeem.* Qum: Imam Hussain (a) Publishing House, 2004.

Al-Hakeem, Muhammad Baqir. *Thawrat Al-Hussain (a).* Najaf, 2008.

Al-Hassani, Hashim Ma'roof. *Seerat Al-A'imma Al-Ithney Ashar*. Beirut: Daar Al-Ta'aruf, 1990.

Al-Haydari, Kamal. *Al-Tawheed*. Daar Al-Sadiqayn, 2000.

Al-Haythami, Ali bin Abi Bakr. *Mujama' Al-Zawaid*. Beirut: Daar Al-Kutub Al-Ilmiyya, 1998.

Al-Hilli, Al-Hassan ibn Yusuf. *Kashf Al-Murad fe Sharh Tajreed Al-I'tiqad*. Qum: Muasasat Al-Nashr Al-Islami, 1996.

Al-Hindi, Ali Al-Muttaqi. *Kanz Al-Ummal*. Muasasat Al-Risala, 1989.

Al-Huwayzi, Abd Ali. *Noor Al-Thaqalayn*. Qum: Ismailian.

Al-Isbahani, Ali ibn Al-Hussain. *Muqatil Al-Talibeen*. Qum: Daar Al-Kitaab, 1965.

Al-Khateeb Al-Baghdadi, Ahmad ibn Ali. *Tareekh Baghdad*. Beirut: Daar Al-Kutub Al-ilmiyya, 1997.

Al-Kulayni, Muhammad ibn Yaqoub. *Al-Kafi*. Tehran: Daar Al-Kutub Al-Islamiya, 1968.

Al-Maghribi, Al-Nu'man ibn Muhammad. *Sharh Al-Akhbar*. Qum: Muassasat Al-Nashr Al-Islami, 1993.

Al-Majlisi, Muhammad Baqir. *Bihar Al-Anwar*. Beirut: Al-Wafaa, 1983.

Al-Mar'ashi, Shihab Al-Deen Al-Najafi. *Sharh Ihqaq Al-Haqq*. Qum: Ayatollah Mar'ashi Najafi Library.

Al-Mas'oudi, Muhammad Fadil. *Al-Asrar Al-Fatimiya*. Rabitat Al-Sadaqa Al-Islamiyya, 1999.

Al-Mufeed, Muhammad ibn Muhammad. *Al-Irshad*. Beirut: Daar Al-Mufeed, 1993.

Al-Muhaqiq Al-Hilli, Ja'far ibn Al-Hassan. *Al-Mu'tabar*. Qum: Mu'assasat Sayyid Al-Shuhada, 1985.

Al-Muqarram, Abdulrazzaq Al-Mousawi. *Maqtal Al-Hussain (a)*. Qum: Daar Al-Thaqafa li Al-Tiba'a wa Al-Nashr, 1990.

Al-Murtada, Ali ibn Al-Hussain. *Tanzeeh Al-Anbiya'*. Beirut: Daar Al-Adwaa', 1989.

Al-Naqdi, Ja'far Al-Rubei'i. *Zaynab Al-Kubra*. Qum: Mu'assasat Al-Imam Al-Hussain, 1991.

Al-Nisa'i, Ahmad ibn Shu'ayb. *Al-Sunan Al-Kubra*. Beirut: Daar Al-Kutub Al-Ilmiyya, 1991.

Al-Nisabouri, Abu Abdullah Al-Hakim. *Al-Mustadrak*. Beirut: Daar Al-Marifa.

Al-Nisabouri, Muhammad ibn Al-Fattal. *Rawdat Al-Waa'ithein*. Qum: Manshoorat Al-Radi.

Al-Qummi, Abbas. *Muntaha Al-Aamaal*. Beirut: Al-Daar Al-Islamiyya, 1994.

Al-Qummi, Ali ibn Muhammad Al-Khazzaz. *Kifayet Al-Athar*. Qum: Al-Khayyam, 1980.

Al-Radi, Muhammad ibn Al-Hussain. *Nahj Al-Balagha*. Beirut: Daar Al-Ma'rifa.

Al-Rawandi, Saeed ibn Hibatallah. *Al-Kharayij*. Qum: Muasasat Al-Imam Al-Mahdi.

Al-Sadouq, Muhammad ibn Ali. *'Ilel Al-Sharai'*. Najaf: Al-Matbaa Al-Haydaria, 1966.

Al-Sadouq, Muhammad ibn Ali. *'Uyoon Akhbar Al-Rida*. Beirut: Al-A'lami, 1984.

Al-Sadouq, Muhammad ibn Ali. *Al-Amaali*. Qum: Muassasat Al-Bitha, 1996.

Al-Sadouq, Muhammad ibn Ali. *Al-Khisal*. Qum: Jama'at Al-Mudarriseen, 1982.

Al-Sadouq, Muhammad ibn Ali. *Ikmal al-Din*. Qum: Muasasat Al-Nashr Al-Islami, 1984.

Al-Sadouq, Muhammad ibn Ali. *Man La Yahtharahu Al-Faqih*. 2nd ed. Qum: Jama'at Al-Mudarriseen.

Al-Sadouq, Muhammad ibn Ali. *Thawab Al-'Amal*. Qum: Muassasat Al-Bitha, 1989.

Al-Sadr, Muhammad. *Tareekh Al-Ghayba Al-Kubra*. Beirut: Daar Al-Taaruf, 1992.

Al-Shaheed Al-Awwal, Muhammad ibn Makki Al-Amili. *Al-Mazar*. Qum, 1989.

Al-Shaheed Zayd ibn Ali ibn Al-Hussain. *Musnad Zayd ibn Ali*. Beirut: Daar Maktabat Al-Hayat.

Al-Subhani, Ja'far. *Mafaheem Al-Quran*. Beirut: Daar Al-Adwaa'.

Al-Subhani, Jaafar. *Fe Thilal Al-Tawheed*. Qum: Muasasat Al-Imam Al-Sadiq, 1991.

Al-Tabarani, Suleiman ibn Ahmad. *Al-Mujam Al-Kabeer*. Daar Ihyaa Al-Torath Al-Arabi.

Al-Tabari, Muhammad ibn Jareer. *Tareekh Al-Tabari*. Beirut, 1983.

Al-Tabatabaei, Muhammad Hussain. *Tafsir Al-Mizan*. Qum: Jama'at Al-Mudarriseen.

Al-Tabrasi, Ahmad ibn Ali. *Al-Ihtijaj*. Najaf: Al-Nu'man, 1966.

Al-Tabrasi, Al-Fadl ibn Al-Hassan. *I'laam Al-Waraa bi A'laam Al-Huda*. Qum: Mu'assasat Aal Al-Bayt, 1997.

Al-Tabrasi, Radi Al-Deen. *Makarim Al-Akhlaq*. Manshurat Al-Shareef Al-Radi, 1972.

Al-Tousi, Muhammad ibn Al-Hassan. *Al-Amaali*. Qum, 1993.

Al-Tousi, Muhammad ibn Al-Hassan. *Al-Ghayba*. Qum: Muasasat Al-Maarif Al-Islamiya, 1990.

Al-Tousi, Muhammad ibn Al-Hassan. *Misbah Al-Mutahajjid*. Beirut: Fiqh Al-Shia, 1991.

Dah'lan, Ahmad ibn Zayni. *Al-Durrar Al-Saniyya*. Istanbul: Eishiq, 1976.

Ibn Abi Al-Hadeed Al-Mutazili. *Sharh Nahj Al-Balagha*. Beirut: Daar Ihya Al-Torath Al-Arabi, 1965.

Ibn Al-Atheer, Ali ibn Abi Al-Karam Al-Shaybani. *Usud Al-Ghaba*. Qum: Ismailiam.

Ibn Al-Sabbagh, Ali ibn Muhammad. *Al-Fusool Al-Muhimma fi Marifa Al-Aimma*. Qum: Daar Al-Hadith, 2001.

Ibn Hanbal, Ahmad. *Musnad Ahmad*. Beirut: Daar Saadir.

Ibn Katheer, Ismail. *Al-Bidaya wal-Nihaya*. Beirut: Daar Ihya Al-Torath Al-Arabi, 1988.

Ibn Shahrashoob, Muhammad ibn Ali. *Al-Manaqib*. Najaf: Al-Matbaa Al-Haydaria, 1956.

Ibn Talha, Kamal Al-Deen Muhammad. *Matlab Al-Sa'ool fe Manaqib Aal Al-Rasool*. Edited by Majid Ahmad Al-Atiyya.

Ibn Tawoos, Ali ibn Moussa. *Fath Al-Abwab*. Maktab Al-I'laam Al-Islami, 1994.

Imam Zayn Al-Abideen (a). *Al-Saheefa Al-Sajjadiyya*. Qum: Muasasat Al-Nashr Al-Islami.

Sharaf Al-Deen, Sadr Al-Deen. *Haleef Makhzoum*. Beirut: Daar Al-Adwaa', 1992.

Made in the USA
Monee, IL
11 August 2023

40804480R00156